From Garden to Table

GROWING & COOKING
VEGETABLES

From Garden to Table

GROWING & COOKING
VEGETABLES

Pamela Thomas

CRESCENT BOOKS
New York

A FRIEDMAN GROUP BOOK

This 1991 edition published by Crescent Books,
distributed by Outlet Book Company, Inc., a Random House Company
225 Park Avenue South
New York, New York 10003

ISBN 0-517-03749-1

FROM GARDEN TO TABLE
GROWING AND COOKING VEGETABLES
was prepared and produced by
Michael Friedman Publishing Group, Inc.
15 West 26th Street
New York, New York 10010

Editor: Melissa Schwarz
Art Director: Jeff Batzli
Designer: Lynne Yeamans
Photo Researcher: Anne K. Price

Typeset by The Interface Group, Inc.
Color separation by Excel Graphic Arts Co.
Printed and bound in Hong Kong by LeeFung-Asco Printers Limited

8 7 6 5 4 3 2 1

DEDICATION

For Bob Mathews

ACKNOWLEDGMENTS

A book is rarely the product of one person's thought and creativity. In the case of this book on vegetables and their life from garden to table, I was helped immeasurably by several people.

For advice on gardening, I especially want to thank my stepfather, Bob Mathews, for sharing his gardening advice—and his garden itself. With regard to recipes, I want to thank my friends John Hadamuscin and Susan Costner for allowing me to reprint their recipes in this book. Both John and Susan are gifted cooks and fine cookbook writers, and it is a treat to be able to focus on their work. I also am very grateful to two other fine "foodies," Rozanne Gold and Waldy Malouf, for sharing their recipes. Rozanne is not only a fine culinary consultant, she is a terrific cook. Waldy Malouf, chef of The Hudson River Club in New York, is one of the most gifted chefs at work today.

I would also like to thank several people at the Michael Friedman Group. Melissa Schwarz, my editor, gave me the opportunity to write this book, and her meticulous guidance and patience was of great help. I would also like to thank Karla Olson, Sharyn Rosart, Liz Sullivan, and Lynne Yeamans for their kindness, professionalism, and sharp eyes.

CONTENTS

—

© Karin Reinhard/FPG International

© Ralph B. Pleasant/FPG International

INTRODUCTION

Unlike a flower or herb garden, the object of cultivating a vegetable garden is to produce food. Therefore, because the vegetable garden is indelicately utilitarian (as opposed to decorative, like a fragrant rose garden), many people think it must be hidden away from view. Some North Americans, particularly, have long held a rather jaded view of the vegetable garden. Historically, many American immigrants—including the original Pilgrims—lived off the earth and considered themselves to be advancing in life if they moved "off the farm."

It seems, too, that the "fruits" of a vegetable garden are looked on with some disdain. In her marvelous essay, "The Social Status of the Vegetable," M.F.K. Fisher remarks upon the lowly status of cabbages, spinach, and leeks among certain snobbish gourmands. She closes with the question: "Who determines, and for what strange reasons, the social status of a vegetable?," but not until she has made it clear that she holds such views to be absurd.

9

© Art Montes de Oca/FPG International

But this snobbishness—this revolt against the more earthy pleasures—seems to be disappearing. In recent years, vegetable gardening has enjoyed renewed popularity, and certainly vegetarian-style eating (that is, cutting down on meats—particularly the red ones) has become more appreciated. With the increasing interest in ecology and healthful eating, younger people have begun to take pride in cultivating their own vegetable gardens. Because many of today's mass-produced vegetables are so tasteless (many North Americans don't even know the incredible flavor—or texture—of a home-grown tomato!), many gardeners wish to grow the delectable old-fashioned varieties for themselves, often foregoing the use of chemicals.

Although vegetable gardening does not have the "intellectual" cachet of herb gardening or the social status of flower gardening, it is enjoying its own renaissance. And what a pleasure it is. You have only to feast on freshly picked corn, munch on a salad of garden greens and sun-warmed tomatoes, or serve your carefully cultivated asparagus to appreciative guests to know the joys of vegetable gardening.

11

— *Part I* —

© Derek Fell

THE VEGETABLE GARDEN

Chapter 1

PLANNING AND CULTIVATING
A VEGETABLE GARDEN

Opposite: A vegetable garden planned with raised beds. Right: Vegetable gardening is one of life's greatest pleasures.

Courtesy of Gardener's Supply

Vegetable gardening is one of life's most sensual pleasures. It includes the pleasures of digging in the soil, watching the colorful vegetables grow, harvesting the rich crop, and then preparing and enjoying delectable vegetable dishes.

Yet, like all forms of gardening, a successful vegetable garden requires thoughtful planning.

A few tools-of-the-trade, including rack, hoe, and boxes to hold other tools or weeds.

© Ann Reilly/Photo/Nats

A FEW BASICS

The first step toward planning any garden is evaluating the site where your garden will grow and the needs of the plants you wish to grow there. You must consider your climate (especially the prevailing temperatures) and the zone in which you live. (See Hardiness Zone Map, page 17.) Gardeners in Toronto will have to plan their gardens—and the timing of their planting—much differently than gardeners in south Georgia. Nevertheless, most vegetables thrive in most parts of North America.

(Certain special vegetables and fruits, such as avocados and citrus fruits, will grow only in warmer parts of the continent.)

Vegetables are categorized as annual, biennial, and perennial. Most vegetables are annuals, or plants that last for one season, and are characterized as tender, half-hardy, or hardy, which reflects the plant's relationship to the prevailing climate. Tender annuals will not tolerate frost or cold weather; half-hardy plants will grow in cooler weather; hardy annuals will survive heavy frost.

Biennials are plants that take two growing seasons to complete their cycle, while perennials grow and reproduce in the

USDA PLANT HARDINESS ZONE MAP

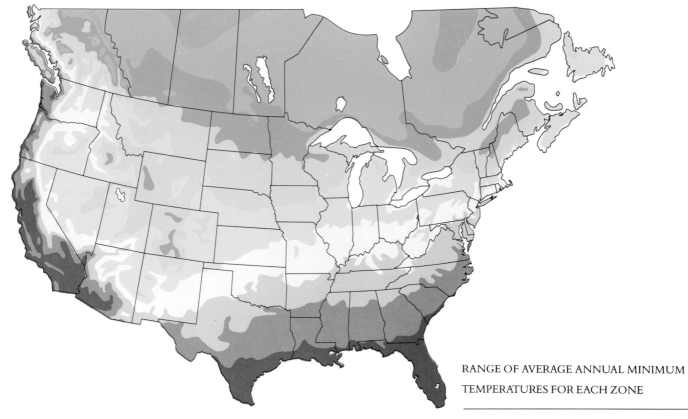

RANGE OF AVERAGE ANNUAL MINIMUM
TEMPERATURES FOR EACH ZONE

ZONE 1	BELOW −50° F	(−45° C)
ZONE 2	−50° TO −40°	(−45° to −40°)
ZONE 3	−40° TO −30°	(−40° to −34°)
ZONE 4	−30° TO −20°	(−34° to −28°)
ZONE 5	−20° TO −10°	(−28° to −23°)
ZONE 6	−10° TO 0°	(−23° to −17°)
ZONE 7	0° TO 10°	(−17° to −12°)
ZONE 8	10° TO 20°	(−12° to −6°)
ZONE 9	20° TO 30°	(−6° to −1°)
ZONE 10	30° TO 40°	(−1° to 4°)

© Derek Fell

A beautifully groomed vegetable garden containing cabbage and lettuce as well as parsley and other herbs.

Since most vegetables are annuals, they grow to maturity within six weeks to three months. Therefore, most vegetables will thrive in North America regardless of whether they are planted in late May or early June (in, say, New England or the Pacific northwest) or March (in, say, southern Louisiana or southern California). On the other hand, days are longer in the North during the summer, and as a result of the increased exposure to the sun, northern plants tend to grow larger and faster.

Sunlight is of primary importance in the vegetable garden, and most vegetables require at least five to six hours of sunlight per day. Nevertheless, some plants require some shade—especially in warmer climates—or at least protection from a hot sun. When planning your garden, consider not only the architectural details of your particular plot, but the normal weather conditions of your area, and select and place your plants accordingly.

The texture and richness of the soil should be considered as well. Most vegetable gardens require some soil preparation to adjust the acidity, provide proper nutrients, and create a texture that allows for adequate drainage. (See Preparing the Soil, page 24). Most vegetables grow best in a loose, rich, loamy soil that is well drained. Soil that contains excessive amounts of clay makes vegetable gardening more difficult, and is hopeless for the root or tuberous vegetables like carrots, beets, potatoes, and leeks.

spring, die down in the autumn, then return the following spring. Biennials and perennials are also evaluated in relation to their ability to survive in particular zones, and since they remain in the earth year after year, their hardiness must be considered carefully. In fact, most vegetables, though they may be biennials or perennials, are cultivated as annuals—with rare exceptions such as asparagus and rhubarb.

18

© Derek Fell

DESIGNING THE GARDEN

Once you have selected your garden site, you must then determine how you will lay it out. Unlike herb gardens that are often designed in intricate, classical forms, vegetable gardens tend to be straightforward. Nevertheless, it is important to think through your plan carefully. Not only can your vegetable garden be a most attractive addition to your garden and yard, but if you plan carefully, you can save yourself hours of labor by placing plants in appropriate areas. Weeds and pests are as eager to feed on vegetables as humans are, and they must be watched for and destroyed.

Also, consider the plants you wish to cultivate. For a vegetable garden, perhaps the most important consideration is the most obvious one: Which plants do you enjoy eating? If you hate the flavor of Swiss chard or cabbage, don't bother planting them. Other plants, like carrots, beets, and celery are so inexpensive at the market, it may not be quite literally worth the effort. On the other hand, certain vegetables like tomatoes, corn, and lettuce, when grown at home, are incomparable to their store-bought sisters. Tomatoes grown for commercial use taste nothing like a home-grown variety picked warm and fresh off the vine. Sweet corn loses flavor literally minutes after it is picked off the stalk. For most amateur gardeners, these vegetables are imperative for a home garden.

19

Think about the amount of time you wish to spend working on your garden. If you are, by necessity or choice, a weekend gardener, think twice about planting a bumper crop of zucchini which by midsummer might take over your entire garden within a day or two—and require extensive weeding besides. Or, if gardening is your passion, experiment with a few unusual plants.

Consider how you plan to use your crops. Do you want to eat all your vegetables immediately? Do you wish to share with friends or neighbors? Do you plan to dry, can, or freeze a large portion of your vegetables for use during the winter months? Limit or expand the size of your garden according to these considerations.

Appraise the appearance of your garden carefully. Will tall plants like corn grow in a position that they will not shade plants that grow closer to the ground? Do large bushes or trees grow nearby that will not only block sun at certain hours, but drain the soil of water and nutrients? Do you wish to add a border of culinary herbs or edible flowers to your vegetable patch?

Before you buy any plants or seeds, thoroughly research your garden conditions, including sunlight, soil, drainage, and the amount of space you have. Then, think about your personal needs, the time you wish to devote to maintenance, and the sorts of foods you wish to eat, whether fresh or preserved.

Drawing a Garden Plan

For best results, it is imperative that you draw a garden plan. First, you'll need to make an accurate drawing of the existing site. Using a grid, measure the outlines of the overall site, and mark immovable fixtures such as fences, patios, large trees, bushes, or buildings. Also note any changes in level that might affect plant growth and therefore require terracing, steps, or raised beds.

Using tracing paper, experiment with different garden plans, taking into consideration the number and kinds of plants you want to grow and the garden's relationship to the rest of the site and the surrounding house or other architectural details. Don't forget to include paths and walkways so that the crops are easily accessible as you plant the garden or harvest your crop. Work out the planting scheme carefully. Appraise the requirements of the plants themselves, taking into account size and, if you are a purist, plant color and plant shapes. Try to plant any perennials (asparagus, rhubarb, and certain culinary herbs) in places where they will not be jostled as they rest over the winter; place delicate plants in spots where they will be safe from children and pets; group plants of the same genus together in one place, or conversely, check to see that certain plants do not inhibit the growth of their neighbors.

Once the soil has been prepared (see page 24), transfer the design to the ground.

Mark the boundaries of the plot with stakes, then mark the beds and paths with string markers, lime, or wood planks.

Purchasing Plants and Seeds

Almost every vegetable (the same is true of fruit) comes in a number of varieties and certain species grow better in some climates than in others. Check with your local garden center, your county Cooperative Extension Service, or even your neighbors to discover which varieties will grow best in your area. (Some seed catalogues will also provide this information.)

Seeds can be purchased at garden centers, hardware stores, florists, and by mail. (See the Mail Order listings on page 124.) Seed packets give planting instructions and are also dated for freshness. (Needless to say, do not buy—or plant—old seeds.) When buying plants, select only those that are healthy looking and appear to have been well tended. Plant them as soon as possible, and keep them in water if they cannot be planted immediately.

Bob Mathews' Garden

The garden on page 22 is a vegetable garden designed by my stepfather, Bob Mathews, who lives in Rocky River, Ohio. Bob grew up on a farm in upstate New York, studied landscape architecture at Syracuse University, and has cultivated a vegetable garden in one form or another every summer of his life. When he retired from business in 1976, he and my mother moved to a smaller house, but with a larger yard— one that Bob could cultivate to his heart's content. He selected this yard because it ran east/west, and therefore had a strong north/south exposure. What's more, the rear yard was not encumbered by any large trees, so his vegetable garden (and his flower garden—which is another story) would have full sun virtually all day long.

The only negative aspect of this plot of land was that the soil contained an excessive amount of clay that hampered drainage. When the land on which their house stands was sold for development, all the topsoil was stripped off. As a result, his rear yard was solid-yellow clay. To create a lawn base, Bob added 1 or 2 inches (2.5 to 5 cm) of topsoil then another inch of peat moss, then he seeded and/or sodded.

For his garden plots, Bob had to work even harder. He enclosed the rear lot with a 36-inch (90-cm) chain link fence, then positioned his vegetable garden on the south lot line, running east and west. The previous owners had already built a bed about 6 inches (15 cm) deep, and 6 feet (180 cm) wide and 20 feet (6 m) long for shrubs, roses, perennials, and annuals, all mixed together seemingly with no master plan. Bob cleared out almost everything, except a large French hybrid lilac that he cut in half, a crab apple tree, and a Burning Bush. (He does not place plants near these since they shade the area and use water and nutrients.)

Bob Mathews' Garden

1. large flowering crab
2. 10-foot (3-m) French hybrid lilac
3. 9-foot (2.7-m) burning bush
4. asparagus
5. strawberries
6. Italian tomatoes
7. table tomatoes
8. early sweet corn
9. late sweet corn
10. green beans
11. black seed, simpson, and buttercrunch lettuce
12. 4 rhubarb plants
13. winter onions
14. 30-foot (9-m) high chainlink fence
15. Miscellaneous annuals, perennials, ferns, and bulbs
16. 8 × 12-inch (20 × 30-cm) railroad ties

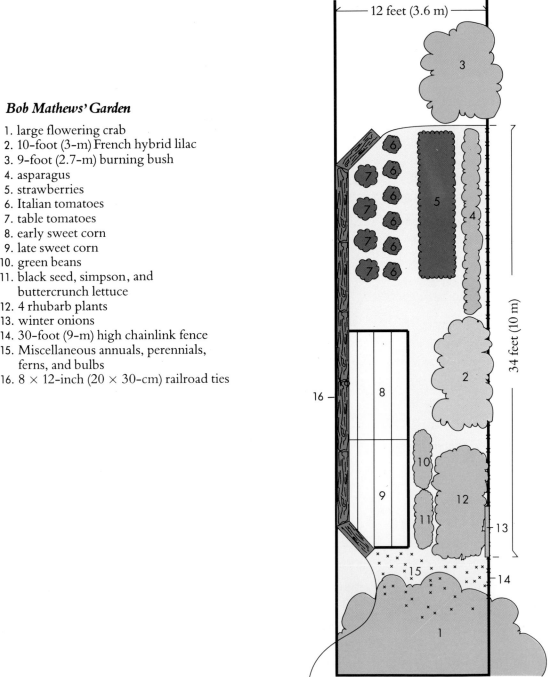

Illustration by William Lombardo

Bob expanded the garden area to 12 feet (3.6 m) wide and 34 feet (10 m) long, and added 8 inches (20 cm) of topsoil. The soil still contained too much clay, so Bob adds straw, horse manure, decomposed leaf mulch, and fall leaves, and tills to about 8 inches (20 cm) deep each fall.

Despite all of this preparation, the soil holds so much water that it cannot be worked until about June 15 most years. Bob lays down boards 10 feet (3 m) long and 10 inches (25 cm) wide so he does not compact the soil by walking on it as he plants. Despite the late planting, Bob has an abundant garden by late summer.

Bob raises only what he and my mother enjoy eating fresh. He claims, "I never raised a good carrot or beet in my life. What's more, both are cheap to buy, and root vegetables don't do well in a clay-based soil. They should have a sandy loam soil so as not to grow forked or stunted." Thus he plants primarily corn, tomatoes, beans, peas, peppers, squash, and lettuce.

With regard to quantity, Bob is also conservative. There are six children in our family, so at one time, Bob cultivated a very ambitious garden. Now, he plants only what "two ancient people" need, as he puts it. His 5 to 6 foot (150 to 180 cm) row of green beans produces more than they eat if they are regularly picked.

Regarding the plan, all the tall plants—corn and tomatoes—are on the north side of the garden where they won't shade lower plants because the sun is south most of the season. His asparagus and rhubarb, planted in 1989, will be ready to eat in 1992. His strawberries, planted in 1990, will produce fruit for two years. Here and there, he plants about a half-dozen broccoli plants. (They don't have to be side by side in a row.)

His Italian tomatoes produce a large pear shaped fruit, excellent for spaghetti sauce or stewed tomatoes. All his tomatoes are staked. Bob usually buys plants early and repots them in 4-inch (10 cm) pots. When they are about 6 inches (40 cm) tall, he digs a trench about 5 or 6 inches (13 or 15 cm) deep and sets his plants with about 8 to 10 inches (20 to 25 cm) remaining exposed.

As soon as his plants are well up, he fertilizes again. He mulches with last fall's leaves picked up with a lawn mower that chops them up somewhat, and frequently does nothing more to them than add fertilizer or insecticides. Although he experimented with organic gardening some years ago, he says he is not a purist.

Bob is not only meticulous, he is down-to-earth, practical and clear thinking. For example, he loathes beets, so he never plants them and, in deference to my mother, also doesn't bother with turnips. Although Bob is an experienced gardener, he describes this particular vegetable garden as appropriate for an avid beginner. He will turn eighty in September, so he designed a plot that would be enjoyable, productive, but a bit easier on the "old" bones.

PREPARING THE SOIL

All vegetables require well-drained soil. If soil retains water for several hours after a rain (or, in general, does not dry out until late spring like Bob Mathews's garden), add organic matter such as a straw-and-manure combination, coarse grit, horticultural sand, gypsum, perlite, or vermiculite to the top 8 to 12 inches (20 to 30 cm) of soil. If the condition appears to be particularly problematic, consider creating raised beds—which is also an advantage if you need to carefully control your soil.

The relative acidity or alkalinity of the soil—the pH factor—is also an important consideration. The pH of soil is a measure of the plants' ability to absorb nutrients, and is measured on a scale of 1 to 14, 1 being the most acidic, 7 being neutral and 14 the most alkaline. To measure the pH of soil, buy a test kit at a garden supply store or have your soil tested at a soil testing lab.

Most vegetables thrive on a somewhat acid soil, or a soil with a pH level of 6 to 7. Also, many fertilizers are slightly acid, so adding them will lower pH somewhat; if you need to further lower the pH, add sulfur or peat moss. On the other hand, if you need to make soil more alkaline, add lime, but only a small amount. Inquire at your local garden center for detailed instructions.

In early spring, you can test the soil's readiness for planting by using the old-fashioned farmer's method: Pick up a handful of soil and squeeze it. If it remains in a tight ball, it is still too wet; if it feels dry and dusty, it needs to be watered deeply for several days before working. If it crumbles easily through your fingers, it is ready to be worked.

Till the area to be worked to a depth of about 12 inches (30 cm). (If you are planting a large plot, you may want to rent a Roto-tiller for a day from your garden center.) If necessary, adjust the pH of the soil, then add fertilizer and, if drainage is a problem, mix in perlite, vermiculite, or another drainage remedy. Once the soil is ready you can sow seeds or plant.

Transplant seedlings with care to insure that the plants are not "traumatized."

PLANTING

Depending upon the plant and your climate, vegetables have a variety of planting requirements. Some can be started from seeds sown directly in the garden, others need to be started indoors and then replanted. Still others are very difficult to cultivate and should be purchased as plants or seedlings.

Starting seeds indoors

Plants with delicate seeds or those that require a long growing season must be started indoors. (Check the individual plant requirements for details.) To start seeds indoors, use flats or small pots, 2 to 4 inches (5 to 10 cm) deep with good drainage holes. Flats and containers can be used from year to year, but must be rinsed thoroughly after each use. You can also use peat pots or fiber containers for plants that do not transplant easily.

Fill the flats or pots with a soilless medium made up of 50 percent peat moss and 50 percent perlite or vermiculite. (Do not use soil or old medium to start seeds since they may be contaminated with disease or old plant material; a sowing medium should always be sterile.) Fill the containers to within 1/4-inch to 1/2-inch (1/2-to 1-cm) of the top, moisten the medium, and sow the seeds. (Check the seed packet for specific sowing directions.)

Cover the flats or pots with clear plastic wrap or glass, and set them in a warm, well-lighted spot.

Once the seeds have germinated, remove the plastic or glass and move the containers into full sun or place them under fluorescent "grow" lights for 12 to 14 hours per day. Water the plants from the bottom as the medium dries out and fertilize the seedlings after they have sprouted about a half-dozen leaves. If you are using flats, transplant seedlings into individual pots when you fertilize.

Before planting the seedlings in the garden, you will need to harden off the plants. (Hardening off means preparing the plants

A cold frame made from old doors and used to "harden off" seedlings.

for their new life in the outdoors.) For about a week before transplanting, move the plants to a protected spot outdoors for several hours during the day, and bring them back in at night. Each day, increase the length of time they remain outdoors. Seedlings can also be hardened off in a cold frame, which is a bottomless box set in the ground with a removable transparent top made of glass or plastic. The temperature in the cold frame is controlled by opening or closing the lid. You can buy a cold frame at your local garden center or make one out of wood and an old storm window. Instructions are available in most basic gardening books.

Starting seeds outdoors

Some plants can be sown directly into the garden, especially those that mature quickly. Smooth and rake the bed, and water slightly. Make furrows, then sow the seeds in rows according to the specific direction for each plant. When plants are 1 to 2 inches (2 to 5 cm) high, thin them to the spacing recommended for that particular plant.

It is important to prepare garden soil meticulously before planting seeds or seedlings.

26

Planting

Some plants are difficult to grow from seed, and should be bought from a garden store instead. Treat store-bought plants as you would your own delicate seedlings. Try to plant them immediately, but if you are unable to put them in the ground right away, place them in pots or flats in partial shade and check them daily to make sure they are receiving sufficient light, warmth, and water.

Plants tend to be shocked when they are first put into the ground, so try to plant in the late afternoon or on a cloudy day to ease the transplanting trauma. Remove the plants from their containers carefully, so as not to disturb the root ball. If plants are in peat pots, peel away as much of the pot as possible and cover the lip of the pot with soil once it is placed in the earth. Water the new plantings daily for about one week or until new growth appears, then water once a week.

After planting, it is sometimes beneficial to add an extra dressing of compost.

© Derek Fell

The vegetable garden should be kept moist. In addition, always water early in the day.

CARING FOR A VEGETABLE GARDEN

Vegetables grow easily, but as a result, a vegetable garden requires time and energy to maintain. Ideally, you should check your garden daily. Certain other life forms are just as eager to feast on the vegetable crop as we are. Check plants carefully for slugs, snails, cutworms, and other pests, and put out appropriate bait. If your garden is plagued by birds, rabbits, raccoons, or other animals, consider adding chicken wire, fences, or traps. These remedies, though perhaps unsightly, will allow your garden to flourish with only a minimum amount of care.

A vegetable garden should be watered at least once a week, although the amount of water needed depends upon the plants and the prevailing weather conditions. For vegetables that like dry soil, allow the soil to dry out between waterings; for plants that like extra-moist conditions, water as frequently as necessary.

When watering, be sure to soak the plants deeply and water those with delicate stems from below. Water plants in the morning so that leaves will dry in the sun. (Leaves that are left wet overnight are susceptible to disease.)

Most vegetables do not require intensive fertilization. Fertilizer put in the soil at planting time is sufficient for a single-crop

© Derek Fell

plant like determinant tomatoes; for those that keep producing throughout the summer, a second fertilization may be necessary in mid-season.

Weeds compete with plants for light, water, and nutrients, and often carry diseases and insects. Some plants even create their own weeds by dropping seeds. Keep the garden weed free by picking flowers before they turn to seed, pulling all other weeds the moment they appear, and mulching.

Mulch is a protective covering that is spread over the soil and around the bases of plants to keep the ground cool and moist, to prevent weeds from sprouting, and to give the garden a more finished look. Organic mulches usually consist of bark chips, leaves, hay, pine boughs, and compost; man-made mulch can be made with black or clear plastic and newspapers. Again, the kind of mulch you select depends upon the individual plants and their needs.

Opposite: Vegetables should be harvested the moment they ripen, preferably in the morning when they are cool.

A Word about Garden Pests and Diseases

Because disease, insects, and other pests are so common in a vegetable garden, it is useful to become familiar with some of the more common ones and know some of the ways to get rid of them. Vegetables, like many garden plants, are susceptible to fungi and bacteria that produce leaf spots, wilts, and root rot. Viruses transmitted by aphids and other pests may result in mottled leaves and stunted plant growth. Insects like aphids, leafhoppers, white flies, spider mites, beetles, and caterpillars may attack plants and destroy leaves and roots. Other pests such as grubs, maggot roundworms, snails, and slugs may also feed on vegetables.

In general, to avoid pests and disease, check leaves and stems frequently for off-color or stunted tissue and remove the "damaged" plants. Always prepare soil properly before planting seeds or plants. Spray plants with water to dislodge insects, other garden pests, and potentially disease-ridden dust and dirt. Allow plants to dry

Vegetable gardens are often prey to pests and diseases. Although some beetles are beneficial, the Colorado potato beetle is one of the bad guys.

off before nightfall and make sure air circulates freely around leaves.

You may wish to use an insecticide or a fungicide for particular problems. Recommended pesticides vary from region to region, so check with your garden center regarding appropriate use in your area. Also, take special care when using insecticides since you are cultivating edible plants. Consult a natural gardening book for ideas on eliminating pests without using chemicals.

HARVESTING VEGETABLES AND HERBS

Perhaps the greatest pleasure in cultivating a vegetable garden is harvesting your crop. Vegetables should be harvested the moment they ripen, so that, some—like beans— will keep producing. Harvest most vegetables in the morning when they are cool. Wash the vegetables in cold water immediately or within minutes of picking them, then refrigerate.

Harvesting herbs is a simple matter: Pick leaves and flowers as soon as they appear.

Edible flowers should be cut as soon as they are fully open—unless you plan to use the buds instead. Put the flowers in water if they are not to be eaten immediately. Remove the stamens, pistils, and the white section at the base of the petals before eating the flower.

WINTERIZING THE GARDEN

In the fall, carefully clear your garden of all dead matter and debris. Mulch any perennial vegetables or herbs that will remain over the winter. Throw old plant material into the compost pile, but check first to be sure it is disease free.

Fantasizing about your garden (in other words, planning for next spring's creation) is half the fun of gardening and allows the gardener to keep working throughout the winter. Keep a gardener's journal and note the placement and quality of your crops. Consider plants you may want to eliminate, reduce, or increase—and think about other plants or new varieties you might want to try. Send for catalogues and seeds. Even gardeners who live in blustery climates can have a long and productive year. Most of all, if you keep some of your crop, you can continue to enjoy it year-round as well.

The vegetable garden in summer (opposite), yielding ripe specimens for the dinner table; and in winter (above), its plants carefully mulched in preparation for cold weather and snow.

33

Chapter 2

GROWING VEGETABLES INDOORS

Opposite: A view from a well-equipped potting shed.

Many people, especially apartment dwellers, simply do not possess a plot of ground in which to create an outdoor garden. Others do not have the time to grow and maintain a full-blown vegetable garden. Nevertheless, they still crave the pleasures of growing food and surprisingly, a vast number of vegetables can be grown in containers—indoors or out. With the exception of various root crops such as beets and turnips, or plants such as cabbage and Brussels sprouts that require extensive space above ground, most vegetables will thrive indoors (or on terraces in containers), including tomatoes, cucumbers, beans, lettuces, radishes, peppers, zucchini, spinach—and even eggplants and melons.

As with a more typical vegetable patch, it is important to select the right varieties for special planting. Seed suppliers will often specify which plants will grow well in containers, and will provide appropriate planning and maintenance instructions.

CONTAINERS

Select a pot that is in proportion to the size of the mature plant you desire to grow—or conversely, select a plant that is appropriate to the container. In addition, consider the environment and appearance of the spot in which the container will be placed.

Containers come in infinite sizes, shapes, and materials. Plastic pots are inexpensive and easy to maintain; unglazed clay pots are more attractive but require more attention since water evaporates from them faster. Larger, more dramatic containers such as wooden tubs require special attention since they can become quite heavy and cumbersome when they are filled with soil.

Only a few vegetables (dwarf cherry tomatoes, for example) are appropriate for cultivation in hanging baskets. However, several varieties of herbs are more suitable, including creeping thyme, ivy, winter savory, rosemary, sage, and some varieties of mint. Remember, too, that plants grown in hanging baskets may need special attention. Some need to be watered quite frequently (as often as once a day), while others may require more sun or will be vulnerable to wind if they are hanging outdoors.

A window box, especially in a sunny kitchen window, can be an ideal place to cultivate a miniature vegetable garden. Like all containers, many kinds of window

boxes are available, from inexpensive, lightweight plastic ones (that tend to crack in cold weather), to clay (which also may crack), to wood. Woodframe window boxes, although sometimes heavy, are attractive and long wearing.

Regardless of your choice of container, all pots need appropriate drainage holes and a

Many vegetables, including lettuce, can be grown in hanging baskets.

layer of gravel, perlite, or broken pottery to prevent water from collecting in the bottom. For smaller containers, use a soilless mixture of peat moss combined with perlite, vermiculite, or coarse sand. For larger containers, mix garden soil with perlite or vermiculite and cultivate the vegetables and herbs as if they were in the garden.

Remember that plants grown in containers need more frequent watering than those grown in the ground. Check the soil daily, especially if it is unusually hot or the plants are situated on a windy balcony or terrace, and bear in mind the needs of the particular plant. For plants that like dry soil, water only when the soil is very dry; for those that like moist soil, water the moment the surface of the soil is dry. Potted plants may also need more fertilizer than garden plants, but be careful not to overfertilize.

POTTING VEGETABLES INDOORS

Pot plants to be grown indoors in the same way you pot them in outdoor containers. Pay special attention to proper drainage and consider setting individual plants in separate pots in a gravel-lined tray as an effective way to ensure sufficient drainage.

As with any potted plant, indoor vegetables require special care, particularly with regard to watering, lighting, and fertilizing. Pots dry out quickly and should be watered, both top and bottom, frequently —every day in hot weather. In addition to direct watering, sufficient moisture in the atmosphere is also important. Spray or mist leaves once or twice a week.

Light is as important as water and special fluorescent lights are available if sunlight is insufficient. Ideally, try to use sunlight during the day and augment with artificial light, if necessary. In addition to needing sun, vegetables grown indoors also require relative warmth and should be kept at a temperature of about 60 to 70 degrees F (16° to 21°C).

Indoor vegetables also need to be fertilized every three or four weeks in spring and summer, and about every six weeks during dormant months. Follow the manufacturer's recommendations carefully.

Indoor vegetables may be susceptible to damage from dust and grease, especially if they are grown in the kitchen. To protect them, spray or mist the herbs frequently to remove dust and wipe larger leaves by hand to remove grease. Remove dead or damaged leaves promptly to encourage growth and discourage disease.

Each vegetable grown indoors has specific needs and requirements. If you choose to cultivate your vegetable garden indoors, get hold of a good general guide to indoor gardening or a specific guide to growing vegetables indoors.

Part II

© Michael Grand

THE VEGETABLES:
FROM GARDEN TO TABLE

Chapter 3

CANNING, FREEZING, AND DRYING VEGETABLES AND HERBS

Opposite: Fruits "stewing" in natural sunlight. Right: Various vegetables beautifully put by.

© Michael Skott

Keeping your produce is one of the hidden challenges of vegetable gardening—and one of the pleasures. Rows of jewel-like bottles of canned tomatoes, beans, or garden fruits inspire a warm and earthy pride. Serving your garden broccoli or your winter squash, planted in May, picked in August, frozen and served at Thanksgiving is surely one of life's great joys.

The methods for preserving foods—storing, canning, freezing, and drying— are ancient and basic.

41

© David M. Stone/Photo/Nats

Strawberries being canned using the hot water bath method.

STORING

The root vegetables, including potatoes, turnips, winter squashes, and onions, can be stored in a root cellar (if you have such a thing) or simply in any cool, dark, dry place. If properly stored, they should last for the entire winter.

CANNING

Canning is a process that seems intimidating at first glance, but is actually quite simple—as long as you follow the rules to the letter.

Basically, there are two methods for canning—the *hot water bath method* and the *pressure cooking method.* The hot water bath method is used for acid foods such as apples, berries, cherries, grapes, and most other fruits. In other words, it is the method used when making preserves, jams, condiments, and juices. Tomatoes are also canned using the hot water bath method.

However, most vegetables (as well as all other nonacid foods) must be canned using the pressure cooking method in order to prevent development of *Clostridium botulinum,* the source of botulism. Even with this canning method, the U.S. Government recommends that all home-canned vegetables should be boiled for 15 minutes in an open pan before testing or tasting.

In addition, the U.S. Government recommends that the following vegetables *not* be canned at home: cabbage (except sauerkraut), cauliflower, celery, cucumbers, baked beans, eggplant, lettuce, onions, parsnips, turnips, and vegetable mixtures.

Both the hot water bath method and the pressure cooking method require specific tools and each vegetable demands particular preparation times. In addition, endless recipes exist for developing tasty canned vegetables, condiments, and preserves. It is beyond the scope of this book to include them here. For detailed directions on the canning processes, consult any good comprehensive cookbook or any specialty book on canning and preserving.

FREEZING

Many vegetables freeze well, including peas, asparagus, green beans, lima beans, broccoli, and corn. (Lettuces, spinach, potatoes, tomatoes, cucumbers, and onions do *not* freeze well.) Sweet potatoes, squashes, celery, and cabbage freeze well, but only if precooked.

To freeze raw vegetables, first select the freshest produce, then in order to stop deterioration, blanch them. More delicate vegetables such as asparagus tips or broccoli florets can be steam blanched, while hardier vegetables such as beans, carrots, or corn can be blanched in water. After blanching, the vegetables must be plunged in ice water, dried thoroughly, then carefully packed in freezer wrap. If they are truly fresh, carefully processed, packaged well (don't forget to label and date your produce), and kept in a reliable freezer (one that maintains a 0°F or -180°C temperature), frozen vegetables will be virtually undistinguishable from fresh vegetables.

Consult a good all-purpose cookbook or a guide to preserving for detailed directions on freezing your harvest of vegetables.

Freezing Herbs

Freezing is a very effective method for preserving herbs. Fragile herbs such as basil, chervil, tarragon, fennel, and chives—tend to lose their flavor when air dried and should always be frozen. In fact, freezing has become an extremely popular way to preserve all culinary herbs because it is fast, easy, and keeps the herbs fresher and more colorful.

To freeze, simply place the herbs in a plastic bag or container, label it, and store in the freezer. Also, consider making herb blends, such as bouquet garni or herbes de Provence mixtures, and freezing them, ready blended.

DRYING

Drying foods is one of the oldest forms of food preservation, and many vegetables—beans, peas, peppers (especially chili peppers), shallots, scallions, and tomatoes—and fruits are delicious dried. Dried vegetables are delicious in soups and stews. As with freezing, pick the vegetables when they are in their prime, blanch them if necessary, then dry them in a home oven, a convection oven, or home drier that can be purchased in a garden store or kitchenware shop. Store them in a cool, dry place. Most will last for at least six months, and in the case of beans or peas for over a year.

The root or tuber vegetables dry better than the leafy vegetables, and in many cases should be blanched before drying. Choose produce that is mature but not overripe or woody. Cut the vegetables into thin, even slices. Pack the dried food immediately in a glass or plastic container, label it, and store it in a cool, dry place.

To rehydrate, immerse the food in water and let it soak until it plumps. Cook rehydrated foods immediately.

For detailed directions consult a good all-purpose cookbook or a book devoted to this subject.

Courtesy of Gardener's Supply

Vegetables in a home dryer.

44

Drying Herbs

The sooner the drying process begins, the better the quality and color the dried herb will be. Drying, however, must be gradual, since if herbs are dried too quickly—such as in an oven—essential oils are lost.

For stemmed herbs such as sage, thyme, or savory, tie a small bunch of herbs together with a string, hang them upside down in a well-ventilated place, then remove the leaves when they have dried. If you are drying small numbers of leaves, lay the leaves out on muslin, cheesecloth, or brown paper and stretch over a rack so that air can circulate around them. Drying racks can be purchased at garden supply centers.

Drying leaves in a microwave oven is a recent innovation and works well. Place leaves or stems between two paper towels and set the oven for about 1½ to 2 minutes. Since drying time varies with each herb, do not combine herb varieties in the drying process. Check drying times frequently.

Storing Dried Vegetables and Herbs

After drying, store vegetables, herbs, and seeds in dark, airtight containers. Store leaves and seeds whole to preserve their flavor; crush them just before using. Label bottles with the name of the herb and date, then store the bottles away from light, heat, moisture, or dust.

Rosemary, sage, parsley, and chives.

© Amy Reichman/Envision

Chapter 4

*Opposite: A lush cauliflower
nestled in its leaves.*

——

GROWING, COOKING, AND KEEPING
26 VEGETABLES

The following vegetables are commonly grown in an average kitchen garden. In addition, a few special vegetables (artichokes, for example) have been added for the more adventurous gardener. Strawberries and rhubarb have also been added because they are both popular and easy to grow. And some herbs and edible flowers are included as well, both to add beauty to the garden and extra flavor to the vegetables themselves. Finally, where appropriate, I've suggested varieties of certain vegetables. (Seed manufacturers frequently cultivate "new" vegetables; check with your garden center or various catalogues to find these more innovative choices or varieties that grow especially well in your area.)

Anyone who has ever grown vegetables at home knows that they are best freshly picked from the garden, and eaten raw or lightly boiled or steamed, served with a light butter sauce. Fresh sweet corn, eaten within hours—or even minutes—of picking, steamed, buttered, and salted, is one of life's great pleasures. Nevertheless, you will find several recipes for traditional sauces here that are delectable on fresh vegetables, as well as some special recipes for preparing garden-fresh vegetables in unusual ways.

© Steven Mark Needham/Envision

A mélange of vegetables — zucchini, broccoli, asparagus, and green beans — sautéed and sprinkled with herbs.

Preparing Cooked Vegetables

A Basic Recipe for 4 servings

Wash, scrape, peel, trim—or otherwise prepare the vegetables. Leave "baby" vegetables whole. Into a heavy saucepan or skillet, place enough vegetables for four people together with 2 or 3 tablespoons of butter and ¼ cup of water. Cover and steam the vegetables until tender. Place the vegetables on a platter and serve. Season with salt, pepper, lemon juice, cheese, or any sauce that suits your fancy.

Preparing Raw Vegetables

A Basic Recipe for a Crudite Platter

A crudite platter can feature as many or as few vegetables as you wish to prepare: artichokes, asparagus tips, whole green beans, snap beans, broccoli florets, carrots (cut in rounds or julienned), cauliflower, cherry tomatoes, new potatoes, beets, celery, finocchio, scallions, snow peas, radishes and zucchini (raw and julienned) are all possibilities. Some vegetables (such as broccoli, carrots, cauliflower, snow peas, and beans) should be blanched briefly and then chilled before serving. Other vegetables (new potatoes, beets) should be cooked through, then chilled and served. Still others need only to be scrubbed, trimmed, and arranged attractively.

Serve raw vegetables with Aioli or any other dip of your choice.

Aioli

Makes about 1 cup

Aioli is a very popular—very classic—sauce that is often served as a dip for crudites or as a sauce for fish, boiled potatoes, or beef.

5 or 6 large cloves garlic, peeled and finely minced
2 egg yolks
Pinch of salt
1 cup olive oil
½ teaspoon water
1 teaspoon lemon juice

In a bowl, place the garlic and the egg yolks, and with a wire whisk, beat until the yolks are a light yellow in color. Beat in the salt, then add the olive oil, dribble by dribble, beating constantly. As the sauce thickens, beat in the water and the lemon juice.

Variation:

If you don't feel like tackling the extensive beating involved in the above recipe, simply beat 2 tablespoons of good olive oil into 1 cup of commercial mayonnaise until well blended. Add the minced garlic, salt, and lemon juice, mix well, and serve.

ARTICHOKES

Maturation: About 160 days

Artichokes are tall, rough looking plants, and the edible part is actually the flower bud. Those who enjoy eating artichokes know that the petals are meaty at the center, and the artichoke heart is a great delicacy—well worth the work of devouring the flower bud itself. Artichoke hearts also make a delicious salad.

© Michael Skott

In the Garden

Artichokes are perennial plants in warm climates—like in Southern California where in fact they grow best in North America—but they can be grown in other climates. Since they require a long growing season, they must be started from root divisions grown indoors.

Start the roots indoors in large (about 3-gallon or 10-liter) containers, then transplant them into rich, well-drained but sandy soil in a sunny area. Plant the root divisions about 3 or 4 feet (90 to 120 cm) apart. Fertilize at planting time and again when the stalks are about 2 feet (60 cm) tall. (They grow to about 5 feet—150 cm—tall.) Harvest in the fall (or winter, in warm climates), when the buds are 3 or 4 inches (8 to 10 cm) in diameter. Cut the buds off with a sharp knife (the stems are thick and tough) about 3 inches (8 cm) below the bud.

In the Kitchen

Artichokes are tricky vegetables to eat, but surprisingly simple to prepare. They are best steamed, and then served hot or cold with a butter or a vinaigrette sauce. Artichoke hearts can be pickled.

Steamed Artichokes with Tarragon Butter Sauce

Makes 4 servings

The following is a very basic recipe for steamed artichokes. They can also be served cold, with other herbed butter sauces, hollandaise sauce (see page 55), a mayonnaise sauce, or a vinaigrette.

4 medium-sized artichokes
1 clove garlic, mashed
1 celery stalk, with leaves
2 tablespoons lemon juice
16 tablespoons (2 sticks) butter
2 tablespoons finely chopped fresh tarragon

Clean the artichokes thoroughly under cool water. Cut off the stalks and the pointed tips at the end of the leaves.

In a large kettle, add the garlic, celery stalk, and lemon juice to about 4 inches (10 cm) of water and bring to a boil. Place the artichokes on a trivet, cover the pot, and allow the artichokes to steam for 45 minutes, or until the leaves are tender and can be pulled apart easily.

Melt the butter in a small saucepan and add the tarragon a few minutes before serving.

Serve hot on a plate, one artichoke per person, with small bowls of the melted butter sauce on the side of each plate.

51

ARUGULA
Maturation: About 45–60 days

Arugula, in a certain sense, belongs with the lettuces. It is a leafy plant, with dark green, tooth-edged leaves, and is intensely flavorful. It is a delightful addition to green salads—in fact, the Tricolore Salad (see page 53)—arugula, endive, and radicchio—has become something of a standard offering in trendy American restaurants.

In the Garden
Arugula, like all salad greens, grows quickly and thus can be planted twice, in early spring (arugula tolerates cooler climates) and again in late summer. Plant seeds in about ½ inch (1 cm) of rich, well-drained soil. To harvest, take the outer leaves, leaving the inner buds to assure further growth.

In the Kitchen
Arugula is delicious, but strongly flavored (some say it has a peanutlike flavor) and the leaves should be mixed with sweeter or milder greens. Sauté arugula as an interesting side dish for virtually any meat entree

Arugula growing in the garden.

© Derek Fell

(roast beef, or roast pork), chicken, or fish (especially monkfish, tuna, or other strong-tasting fish).

Arugula is one vegetable—like many other salad greens, that is not a good choice for preserving in any way—canning, freezing, or even drying. Nevertheless, do not allow this to deter you from adopting arugula for your garden; simply plant only the amount you will use fresh.

52

© Steven Mark Needham/Envision

A tricolore salad made with radicchio, endive, and watercress.

Tricolore Salad

Makes 6 servings

18 arugula leaves (or one mature plant)
1 head of radicchio
2 to 3 Belgian endives
3 tablespoons balsamic vinegar
½ cup extra-virgin olive oil
2 cloves garlic, peeled and minced
1 tablespoon grainy mustard
1 teaspoon sugar

Wash the arugula and the radicchio thoroughly, tear into bite-sized pieces, and dry. Wash the endive carefully and separate the leaves. (If you prefer, you can cut the endives lengthwise into a fine julienne.) Toss the vegetables in a large bowl.

In a cup or bowl, combine the vinegar, olive oil, garlic, mustard, and sugar, and mix together using a fork or small whisk. Dress the salad just before serving.

ASPARAGUS
Maturation: 2 to 3 years

Asparagus is one of the more difficult vegetables to cultivate, but anyone who has feasted on young, spring shoots, lightly steamed and served with any one of many sauces—or just plain—knows that growing asparagus is well worth the effort. Asparagus is a perennial plant that needs to be sown 2 or sometimes 3 years (seasons) before it can be harvested. It grows best in colder climates and is almost impossible to cultivate in warm climates.

In the Garden
Asparagus can be grown from seeds, but usually it is best cultivated from crown or root divisions. Plant in late spring, setting seeds or divisions 15 to 18 inches (38 to 45 cm) apart in rich, well-drained soil. For the first 2 or 3 seasons, allow the stalks to grow, produce foliage, and die back. Harvest in the second or third season (third is better, since it allows the roots to develop fully), but limit the harvest to 3 to 4 weeks, then allow the plants to flower and die back. To harvest, snap off stalks (bend the stalks until they break) or cut, using a small knife or an asparagus knife designed for the purpose. Stalks are best when they are 6 to 8 inches (15 to 20 cm) high.

In the Kitchen
Asparagus is many gourmands' favorite vegetable; in fact, many people consider it a delicacy. It is probably safe to say we will never hear an American president say he does not like asparagus. It is often served as an appetizer either hot or cold (with a hollandaise [see page 55] or vinaigrette sauce) since its unique flavor stands on its own. Or serve it as a side dish with spring lamb, chicken, or fish. It is a vegetable that stands up well in soups, stews, and casseroles, but since the tips are particularly tasty, it is best to serve them fresh, as is, and save the ends for soups and casseroles.

You can freeze and can asparagus.

Hollandaise Sauce

Makes 6 servings (About 1 cup)

Hollandaise sauce can be made in many different ways. It's a tricky sauce to make and much depends upon watching the sauce carefully so that the eggs and cream do not curdle.

4 egg yolks
2 tablespoons heavy cream
1 tablespoon lemon juice
¼ teaspoon salt
¼ teaspoon cayenne pepper, nutmeg, or paprika
(depending upon your taste or the vegetable you
are serving)
16 tablespoons (2 sticks) unsalted butter, softened

In the top of a double boiler, place the egg yolks, cream, lemon juice, salt, and pepper (or other spice). Set the pan over boiling water, and beat the mixture with a whisk until it begins to thicken. Slowly beat in the butter, a little bit at a time. When all the butter has been added, turn off the heat, and continue to whisk until the sauce has thickened. Serve at once.

© Bill Margerin/FPG International

Asparagus, freshly steamed.

Lemon Pasta with Asparagus and Herbs

Makes 4 servings

This incredibly delicious pasta dish is served in New York's world-famous Rainbow Room at Rockefeller Center.

Topping:

Grated rind of 1 lemon
1 tablespoon chopped fresh parsley
1 tablespoon chopped fresh chives
1 tablespoon chopped fresh basil
1 tablespoon chopped mint

16 asparagus spears
8 tablespoons (1 stick) butter, cut into small pieces
1 pound pasta (spaghetti, fettuccine)
1 cup dry white wine
1 tablespoon finely chopped shallots
Juice of 2 lemons
Grated rind of 2 lemons
3 cups heavy cream
3 tablespoons grated Parmesan cheese

In a small bowl, combine the lemon rind, parsley, chives, basil, and mint for the topping. Set aside.

Sauté the asparagus spears in 2 tablespoons of butter until tender. Set aside, but keep warm.

© Thomas Lindley/FPG International

Left: Baby asparagus shoots. Opposite: Pasta with an asparagus and herb sauce.

In a large pot, boil water and cook the pasta until it is al dente. (Follow package cooking instructions.)

As the pasta is cooking, create the sauce: In a heavy saucepan, bring the white wine and the shallots to a boil and simmer until the wine is reduced by half. Strain and return the wine to the saucepan. Add the lemon juice, lemon rind, heavy cream, and cheese. Bring to a simmer and cook slowly, whisking constantly until the sauce has thickened.

Drain the pasta and return to the large pot. Toss the hot pasta with the remaining butter. Add the asparagus and the sauce, and toss until pasta is coated. Place pasta in serving bowl or platter, sprinkle with the topping and serve immediately.

BEANS

Beans are one of the most common occupants of a vegetable garden and, like squash, come in a number of different sizes, shapes, and varieties. Broad beans, snap beans (or string beans), and lima beans are a few of the types frequently grown.

Broad Beans
Maturation: About 85 days

Broad beans or fava beans grow on tall, thick stems and produce large pods that can be as much as a foot (30 cm) long. When the pods are young—3 to 4 inches (8 to 10 cm) long—the entire pod can be eaten like a snap bean, but normally the seeds, which are about the size and shape of lima beans and are buried inside the pods, are the favored food.

In the Garden
Plant seeds in a sunny place in rich, well-drained soil. Set seeds about 1 inch (2.5 cm) deep, 10 inches (25 cm) apart, in rows about 3 feet (90 cm) apart. The rugged stems usually require a pole, stake, or trellis for support. Harvest the pods after about 60 days

A basket containing three varieties of green beans.

or pick the pods after 90 days and shell the seeds.

In the Kitchen
Broad beans or fava beans are eaten interchangeably with lima beans or snap beans. They make a nice side dish with stronger flavored meats like beef or pork and the seeds are tasty in soups and stews. Whole pods or shelled seeds are best steamed or boiled.

Fordhook lima beans ready to be harvested.

Lima Beans
Maturation: About 70 days

Lima beans are the kidney-shaped beans traditionally used by mothers to seemingly torture small children. However, many adults grow up to like these sweet, hearty beans, which can serve as a substitute for potatoes or rice since they are a good source of carbohydrates. Several varieties of lima beans exist, some pole (or vine) varieties (such as King of the Garden) and some bush varieties (such as Fordhook 242).

In the Garden
Lima beans require a sunny, warm position in the garden and should be planted in late spring. Set seeds 3 inches (8 cm) apart in about 2 inches (5 cm) of well-drained soil. When plants reach about 6 inches (15 cm) in height, thin them to about 6 inches (15 cm) apart and pole if necessary. Unlike broad beans, lima beans must be shelled before cooking no matter when they are harvested.

In the Kitchen
Some people think lima beans have a sweet flavor; others find them nutty. It is a heartier bean than the snap bean, probably because it contains more sugar. Lima beans make an excellent side dish for most beef, chicken, or fish dishes—and a nice addition to soups and stews. Lima beans also puree well and make a nutritious baby food.

Snap Beans
Maturation: About 60 days

Snap beans or string beans are what we commonly think of as green beans, although they come in yellow and purple varieties. Like other members of the bean family, some are pole beans and others are bush beans. Snap beans are one of the most versatile garden vegetables; they grow relatively easily in most climates and are a healthy and delicious food.

In the Garden
In cooler climates, start seeds indoors in peat pots and transplant after the last frost, or plant seeds in late spring. Place seeds about 1 inch (2.5 cm) deep, 2 inches (5 cm) apart in rows about 12 inches (30 cm) apart. For pole or vine plants, plant 3 or 4 seeds per pole, then as vines mature, thin to the single strongest plant. (Insert poles or trellises before seeding.) To make sure that you have fresh beans throughout the season, plan two or three plantings, at 3- or 4-week intervals. Since the beans take only about 60 days to mature, they can be planted as late as July for an early September crop.

Harvest when the beans are large enough to eat, or about 5 inches (13 cm) long.

In the Kitchen
Snap beans get their name from the sound they make when broken in half. Eat them raw (or blanched) as a crudite or serve cold in a vinaigrette sauce as an appetizer. Beans are also a fine addition to a green or pasta salad as well as to soups, or stews. Of course, as a side dish you can serve them lightly steamed. French-style green beans are sometimes imitated by slicing beans in half lengthwise. True French green beans are difficult to obtain in North America.

To preserve, can or freeze green beans. Both processes change the texture of the beans, while canned beans have a distinctly different flavor than fresh.

Snap Beans in Cream with Parsley and Dill

Makes 6 servings

2 pounds fresh snap beans
4 tablespoons (1/2 stick) butter
Salt
Freshly ground pepper
1 tablespoon chopped fresh dill
1 cup heavy cream
2 tablespoons chopped fresh parsley

Wash the beans carefully, trim the ends, and remove any traces of string. If they are tender, cook whole; otherwise cut on a diagonal.

© J. Baker/FPG International

Freshly steamed snap beans.

Bring a pan of salted water—enough to cover the beans—to a boil and add the beans in batches. Boil for a few minutes, then reduce heat to medium and cook for 12 to 15 minutes. The beans should be crisp but not raw. Drain the beans and return them to the saucepan with the butter. Add salt and pepper to taste. Add the dill and cream, and toss with the beans. When the beans are well coated with cream sauce, spoon into a heated serving dish and sprinkle them with the parsley.

BEETS
Maturation: About 60 days

Beets are an interesting garden vegetable, not only because of their beautiful red color (which can also be purple, yellow, or white), but because their leaves (particularly their early seedling leaves) provide an interesting addition to salads and soups. Since they are primarily a root vegetable, beets do not grow well in clay soil, and if grown there, will probably be small and deformed.

In the Garden
Plant seeds in early spring in rich, loamy (i.e. nonclay), well-drained soil. Place seeds about 2 inches (5 cm) apart in about ¼ inch (½ cm) of soil, then thin seedlings to about 4 inches (10 cm) apart. Continue to sow seeds about once a month until about 8 weeks before the last frost for a continuous crop. To harvest, pull up roots when they are about 3 inches (8 cm) in diameter.

In the Kitchen
Not everyone loves beets, but for those who have cultivated a taste for them, they provide a multitude of pleasure. The vivid purple and red color of beets visually enhances salads and crudite platters. (Beets tend to bleed, so bear that in mind when preparing your salad.) And of course, beets are delicious in soups (borscht being the most well known) and are also excellent served warm as a side dish with pork, beef, tongue, or smoked fish.

Beets can be frozen, but should first be boiled, the skins removed, and then packed in plastic freezer bags. Beets are also delicious pickled or canned.

Beet and Endive Vinaigrette with Swiss Chard

Makes 4 servings

1 pound (4 or 5) beets
2 Belgian endives, washed
½ cup olive oil
2 cloves garlic, peeled and mashed
3 tablespoons tarragon vinegar
1 tablespoon grainy mustard
Several leaves of Swiss chard, washed and chilled

Wash the beets thoroughly, then boil in salted water until tender, cool slightly, then slip off the skins. Set aside until thoroughly cooled, then slice into a thin julienne.

Wash the endive heads in cold water, then slice crosswise into a thin julienne.

In a large bowl, combine the olive oil, garlic, vinegar, and mustard and thoroughly combine using a fork or small whisk. Add the sliced beets and endive and toss until the vegetables are thoroughly covered with the dressing. Chill.

Serve on individual salad plates on a few leaves of Swiss chard.

Very young "Detroit Dark Red" beets.

BROCCOLI
Maturation: About 85 days

Despite President Bush's denigrating remarks, broccoli is many people's favorite vegetable. It is a pretty vegetable in the garden with its thick stems, flower heads, and generous leaves. And it is an attractive vegetable at the table, whether served as a vibrant-green side dish or as an attractive addition to a crudite platter.

In the Garden
Since broccoli requires a long growing season, it is best to buy plants or start seeds indoors in late winter or early spring. They will tolerate cold, so they can be set outside before the last frost. Space plants about 2 feet (60 cm) apart in rows about 3 feet (90 cm) apart in rich, well-drained soil. (For an autumn crop, replant in midsummer.) Keep soil moist and cool, and depending upon the soil, broccoli may need more fertilizing than other garden vegetables. To harvest, cut the head at the stem.

In the Kitchen
Broccoli is a versatile vegetable. Steamed and served with a plain butter sauce, it makes an attractive and delicious accompaniment to beef, lamb, pork, chicken, and fish. With its vibrant color and lovely shape, it looks pretty on a plate. Like asparagus, it is enhanced by sauces, such as hollandaise, and when steamed and arranged attractively can serve as an appetizer.

Broccoli cans reasonably well, and freezes beautifully.

Freshly steamed broccoli, ready to be eaten.

64

Cheese and Broccoli Tart in an Herbed Pastry Crust

Makes one 9-inch (23-cm) tart

Pastry shell:

1 cup all-purpose flour, unsifted
½ teaspoon salt
8 tablespoons (1 stick) butter, chilled
1 egg yolk
1 tablespoon cold water
1 tablespoon fresh herbs (tarragon, dill, oregano, marjoram, or parsley—or mixture of herbs)

Cheese and Broccoli Filling:

½ pound fresh broccoli
½ pound Swiss cheese
2 tablespoons butter
2 tablespoons minced onion
6 egg yolks
Salt to taste
Freshly ground black pepper to taste
1½ cups heavy cream

Preheat oven to 450 degrees F (232°C).

To make the pastry shell, place the flour and salt in a small bowl. Make a well in the center, and slice in the cold butter. Add the egg yolk, water, and herbs. With your hands, squeeze the ingredients into a paste, then knead until all the ingredients are incorporated into a rough dough.

Roll the dough out in a circular shape until it is about 1 inch (2.5 cm) larger than a 9-inch (23-cm) pie plate. Gently place the dough onto the pie plate, letting it cover the bottom and sides loosely. Pat it gently into place with your fingers. Fold the overhanging edge under itself making a double edge of dough. Flute the edge. Prick the bottom and sides of the pie shell with a fork.

Bake in the center of the preheated oven for 8 to 10 minutes until pastry is set and begins to brown. Remove from oven and cool.

Wash, trim, dry, and chop the broccoli. Grate the cheese. Set aside.

In a skillet, melt butter and sauté the onions and broccoli over moderate heat for 5 minutes. Remove from heat and spread the onion and broccoli mixture over the bottom of the partially baked pie crust. Sprinkle the shredded Swiss cheese over the vegetables.

Place the egg yolks in a small bowl. Add the salt, and pepper, and stir. Gradually beat in cream.

Preheat oven to 350 degrees F (177°C). Place the prepared crust on a baking sheet and pour in the egg and cream mixture. In the center of the oven, bake the tart until it is barely set in the center, about 35 or 40 minutes. Remove from the oven and cool slightly. Serve warm.

CABBAGE

Maturation: About 75 days

The sight of large, firm heads of cabbage lined up in a garden is a special delight. Several varieties are available with the most common being Early Jersey Wakefield, Red Acre, and Savoy Ace. Cabbage grows well in cooler weather (and soil) and thus can be cultivated throughout the winter in the South and from early spring to late fall in the North.

In the Garden
It's best to either buy cabbage plants or start seeds indoors, and then plant them in the garden. Set plants in moist, loamy, well-drained soil, about 18 inches (45 cm) apart, in rows about 24 inches (60 cm) apart. Fertilize at planting time and once again during the growing season, and keep the soil moist. Mulch the surrounding soil to keep it sufficiently cool. Harvest heads when they are round and firm.

In the Kitchen
When cooks think of cabbage, it usually evokes images of sauerkraut, cole slaw, and stuffed cabbage, staples of many middle-European cuisines. In recent years, contemporary cooks have experimented with new ways to prepare these "mundane" dishes, and the results have been spectacular. (For example, try the Stuffed Cabbage, page 68.)

The only recommended method for preserving cabbage is "brining"; in other words, making sauerkraut. (Cabbage should not be canned, and does not freeze well.) Making sauerkraut at home is time-consuming and tricky, and hardly worth the effort since it is inexpensive to purchase ready made.

Opposite: Bok choy or Chinese cabbage. Above: Savoy cabbage growing beautifully in the garden.

67

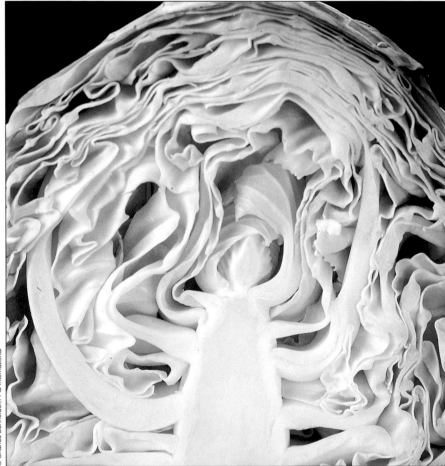

**A crisp cabbage head, sliced
in half.**

Cabbage Stuffed with Mushrooms, Walnuts, and Bulgur

Makes 6 servings

This recipe developed by Susan Costner in her book *Good Friends, Great Dinners*, elevates the mundane stuffed cabbage to a delicacy. She recommends using Savoy cabbage to create the "best-looking" results, but the recipe is just as tasty using any variety.

1 large head cabbage, outer leaves removed
3 tablespoons unsalted butter
1 clove garlic, peeled and minced
1 bunch scallions, finely chopped
2 celery stalks, finely chopped
1 pound fresh shiitake mushrooms or white button
 mushrooms, coarsely chopped
2 cups bulgur, cooked according to package
 directions
⅓ cup finely chopped fresh parsley
2 tablespoons chopped fresh dill
Salt and freshly ground black pepper to taste
¼ cup walnuts, toasted for 10 minutes at 350°F
 (177°C), then coarsely chopped
6 cups Tomato-Caraway Coulis (recipe follows)
½ cup dairy sour cream
Dill or fennel sprigs

Cut out the deep core of the cabbage and discard it. Bring a large pot of salted water to a simmer. Add the cabbage and cook until you can easily remove the largest leaves, about 5 minutes. Remove from the pot and drain well. Carefully separate twelve of the largest leaves and, if not soft enough to roll easily, return them to the pot and cook until tender. Cut out the tough central rib of each leaf. Pat dry and set aside.

Melt the butter in a medium-sized skillet, add the garlic, scallions, and celery, and sauté until just tender. Add the mushrooms and sauté over medium heat, stirring frequently, until all the liquid has been released and then evaporated from the mushrooms. Add the cooked bulgur, parsley, dill, salt, and pepper. Stir in the toasted walnuts and heat thoroughly.

Place the cabbage leaves, curly-side up, on a clean flat surface. Fill with 3 to 4 tablespoons of stuffing. Fold up bottom edge. Fold in both sides and roll up toward top edge. Place, seam-side down, in one layer in a large casserole. Add Tomato-Caraway Coulis and simmer gently for 30 minutes.

Serve the stuffed cabbage, accompanied by some of the sauce. Garnish with sour cream and dill or fennel sprigs.

Tomato-Caraway Coulis

Makes 6 cups

½ small onion, finely chopped
2 cloves garlic, peeled and minced
2 tablespoons unsalted butter
1 tablespoon olive oil
4 cups coarsely chopped, canned, drained Italian
  plum tomatoes
¼ teaspoon sugar
1 bay leaf
2 teaspoons caraway seeds
One 1-inch piece orange peel
1 tablespoon tomato paste
Salt and freshly ground black pepper to taste

In a saucepan, sauté the onion and garlic in the butter and olive oil until tender. Be careful not to brown them. Stir in the tomatoes, sugar, bay leaf, caraway seeds, and orange peel. Cook, covered, over low heat for 10 minutes; then uncover, add the tomato paste, and cook for 10 to 15 minutes more. Discard the bay leaf and orange peel after cooking. Use the coulis as is, or force through a food mill. Correct the seasoning with salt and pepper.

CARROTS
Maturation: About 60 days

Carrots are so inexpensive to buy in the grocery store and in some areas so difficult to grow (particularly in clay soil), think carefully before taking up space in your garden with the "lowly" carrot. Nevertheless, pulling the first bright orange root from the soil is an almost childlike delight. And, like all homegrown vegetables, a carrot from your own garden, if it has grown well, will be sweeter than any you could possibly buy.

In the Garden
Carrots mature relatively quickly, so sow seeds in the garden as early in spring as possible. For a continuous supply, make successive plantings every 3 or 4 weeks. Plant seeds about ¼- to ½-inch (½- to 1-

cm) deep, then after germination, thin plants, if necessary, to about 2 inches (5 cm) apart in rows about 8 inches (20 cm) apart. Carrots grow best in loose, sandy soil; for this soil consider Danvers or Tendersweet varieties. If your soil is heavier, consider one of the "short" varieties, such as Little Finger or Short 'n' Sweet.

In the Kitchen
Like celery and onions, carrots are virtually a kitchen basic. They are eaten raw or cooked; they are used in soups—or can be pureed into a carrot soup; they are a classic side dish with traditional roast beef, pork, lamb, or chicken; and, because they contain natural sugar, are sometimes even used in cookies and cakes. (Carrot cake is a perennial favorite for many people.)

Carrots are also easy to preserve. They can, freeze, or dry well as is. They can also be cooked, pureed, and canned or frozen.

Freshly harvested carrots.

Sugar and Spice Carrots

Makes 6 servings

My grandfather used to tell us that when he was a little boy living in Saugus, Massachusetts, at the turn of the century, his grandmother forced him to eat pulpy carrots from her garden—and he hated them. For over eighty years, he avoided eating carrots, but when he was served these—just after he turned ninety—he ate them with pleasure. You will, too.

2 pounds whole baby carrots, scrubbed and peeled
4 tablespoons (¹/₂ stick) unsalted butter
3 tablespoons dark brown sugar
¹/₂ teaspoon ground ginger
¹/₂ teaspoon ground cinnamon
¹/₂ teaspoon ground nutmeg

Place the carrots in a saucepan with water to cover. Simmer 'til just tender, about 10 to 12 minutes. Drain and set aside.

In the same saucepan, melt the butter. Add the brown sugar and the seasonings, then add the carrots and toss them in the sugar and spice mixture for 2 or 3 minutes or until the carrots have caramelized. Serve immediately.

© Judd Pilossof

Cooked carrots with an herb and butter sauce.

71

Chicken Soup with Vegetables

Makes 6 to 8 servings

This is not a very glamorous recipe, but it is simple, tasty, and one that can be easily adjusted to serve all sorts of purposes—including finding a home for leftovers. I particularly like this soup cooked with an abundance of carrots.

4 large chicken breasts, skin removed
8 cups water
4 medium-sized white onions, whole
Salt and freshly ground black pepper to taste
2 cups chopped celery
4 to 6 large carrots, peeled and sliced crosswise
2 cups fresh green peas
2 tablespoons herbes de Provence (see page 120)

Place the chicken breasts, water, onions, salt, and pepper in a large kettle and bring to a boil. Reduce the heat and simmer for about 30 minutes. Skim any fat off the top of the stock as it rises.

Add the celery and carrots, and cook for 15 minutes. Add the peas and cook for 10 to 15 minutes more, or until the peas are cooked through.

Remove the chicken breasts from the kettle and pull the meat from the bone, shredding it into bite-sized pieces as you debone it. (The meat should fall easily from the bone.) Place the meat in a soup tureen, add

the vegetable soup, and serve with crackers or crusty bread.

Note: I often use this method to cook chicken. When the chicken is cooked, I remove the breasts, wrap them in plastic wrap, and refrigerate them for use in salads or other dishes, then eat the vegetable soup that's left.

A simmering pot of chicken and vegetable soup.

Cream of Vegetable Soup

Makes 6 to 8 servings

Sometimes the hodgepodge of vegetables from the Chicken Soup with Vegetables, though delicious, results in a rather unattractive mélange. If so—or if you prefer a heartier, creamier pureed vegetable soup— try the following. (If you use lots of carrots, your creamed soup will be a lovely orange color.)

1 recipe for Chicken Soup with Vegetables
*   (see page 72)*
1 cup heavy cream
1 to 2 tablespoons chopped chives

   Remove the chicken breasts, wrap them in plastic wrap, and refrigerate for another dish. Place the vegetables and the broth in a blender and liquify until the vegetables are smooth. Return the puree to the kettle and reheat. Add the heavy cream and cook until the soup is hot. Serve immediately, garnished with chopped chives.

Note: This soup is also delicious served cold. After pureeing the vegetables, chill them. Just before serving, whisk in the cream and garnish with chives. Or, instead of adding cream, place a dab of sour cream on top of each serving of the chilled vegetable puree.

© Steven Mark Needham/Envision

Cream of vegetable soup with lots of chunky vegetables.

73

CORN

Maturation: 60 to 90 days

Certain "modern" varieties of corn claim to retain their sweetness for up to two weeks, but purists maintain that for truly delicious corn, the ears must be steamed and served within minutes—or certainly hours—of picking. Many farmers rush their freshly picked ears to neighbors who delight in the sweetness of corn. One definition of a "feast" for many people is a meal of sweet corn and tomatoes picked just minutes before serving.

In the Garden

Plant seeds in rich, well-drained soil in late spring after the last frost has occurred and the soil has warmed. Plant seeds about 2 inches (5 cm) apart, in rows about 2 feet (60 cm) apart, then thin the seedlings to about 12 inches (30 cm). To ensure pollination (and sufficient crop, even for a small family), plant at least three rows of twelve plants each. Some home gardeners stagger their planting (planting seeds 1 to 2 weeks apart) and create two or three crops to ensure sufficient supply during the last weeks of summer. Harvest when the ears are firm and the silk is thick and brownish; break ears from the stalk, taking a bit of the stem.

In the Kitchen

Sweet corn, steamed within minutes of picking, and served with butter and salt is, of course, the quintessential method of serving it. The next best thing to picking it from your own garden is buying it from a garden stand with the corn field in full view in the distance.

In any case, corn is one of the most versatile vegetables. Corn bread, corn pudding, corn chowder, and corn fritters are all classics. As a side dish, scraped from the cob and/or creamed, corn can substitute for potatoes or rice. Its bright-yellow color and interesting texture make it a fine addition to salads and soups.

Corn cans and freezes extremely well.

Corn on the cob nestled in its husks.

74

Corn Bread Hernando

Makes one 9- × 9-inch (23- × 23-cm) loaf

Hernando Courtright was a famous hotel-
ier, owner of the Beverly Hills Hotel and
later the Beverly Wilshire in Los Angeles.
He loved the Mexican culture, and since
this recipe has a Latin flavor it is dedicated
to him.

1¼ cups stone-ground yellow corn meal
1 cup unbleached all-purpose flour
⅓ cup sugar
1 tablespoon baking powder
¼ teaspoon baking soda
½ teaspoon salt
1 large egg
1 cup buttermilk
4 scallions, minced
⅓ cup chopped green pepper
1 cup corn kernels
6 tablespoons (¾ stick) unsalted butter, melted

Preheat the oven to 400 degrees F
(23° C).

In a large bowl, combine the corn meal,
flour, sugar, baking powder, baking soda,
and salt. In a small bowl, whisk the egg then
beat in the buttermilk. Add the buttermilk
mixture to the dry ingredients and stir. Add
the scallions, peppers, corn, and butter and
stir until all the ingredients are combined.

Pour the batter into a 9- × 9-inch
(23- × 23-cm) cake pan, and bake for about
30 to 35 minutes or until the top turns
golden brown. Remove from heat and serve
while hot.

*Classic Corn Bread cut into
ready-to-eat squares.*

75

CUCUMBER
Maturation: About 60 days

Cucumbers—and cucumber vines—come in many varieties. Some vines produce male and female flowers; some vines self-pollinate and produce seedless fruits; some cucumbers are for salads (Bush Crop, Sweet Slice) and some are for pickling (County Fair 87, Earli-pick). As with carrots and celery, one might think cucumbers are more easily purchased than grown, but, again, there is nothing sweeter than a homegrown cucumber.

In the Garden
Plant seeds or seedlings in rich, light, well-drained soil. Sow seeds about 1 inch (2.5 cm) deep, about 6 inches (15 cm) apart, in rows about 3 feet (90 cm) apart. Cucumber vines can be staked or trellised, or can be allowed to spread over the ground. Harvest cucumbers when they are 6 to 8 inches (15 to 20 cm) long. Like beans, cucumbers should be harvested frequently to ensure continuous growth.

Cucumbers grown for pickling are cultivated in the same way. Pick them when they are 1 to 8 inches (3 to 20 cm) long, depending upon their variety.

© Jim Hamel/FPG International

In the Kitchen
Unlike certain other vegetables, cucumbers have relatively few uses from a culinary point of view. Nevertheless, despite their limited range, they hold a very special place in the hearts (and taste buds) of much of the world's population. Where would Middle Easterners be without cucumber salads; where would middle Europeans be without dill pickles; and where would Midwestern ladies be without cucumber sandwiches? Actually, many different cold soups, salads, and pickles can be created with cucumbers.

Cucumbers should be harvested while they are young (about 50 to 60 days from planting) and picked every other day.

Garden Gazpacho

Makes 6 servings

3 cucumbers
1 green pepper
8 ripe tomatoes
1 large Bermuda onion, chopped
2 cloves garlic, peeled and smashed
¼ cup red wine vinegar
½ cup olive oil
Salt to taste
Freshly ground black pepper

Peel, seed, and chop two of the cucumbers; seed and chop the pepper. Chop six of the tomatoes. Place the chopped cucumbers, the pepper, half the chopped onion, the garlic, and the chopped tomato pieces into a blender and puree. Pour the blended vegetables into a bowl and stir in the vinegar, olive oil, salt, and pepper, and chill thoroughly.

Coarsely chop the remaining cucumber, and place it in a small bowl; place the remaining chopped onion in another bowl, and the remaining tomatoes, chopped, in a third bowl.

Serve the soup thoroughly chilled. Pass the chopped vegetables for garnishes.

© George Mattei/Envision

A delicious mix of tomatoes, zucchini, onions, and garden herbs in a soup served cold, gazpacho is truly a garden-to-table dish.

LETTUCES
Maturation: Varies according to variety

Lettuce comes in many varieties, and each possesses special needs with regard to cultivation. Check with your garden center or other gardeners in your area to see which varieties grow best in your climate. Also, when considering salad greens, think about adding arugula, radicchio, curly endive, Swiss chard, and spinach to your garden.

Here are a few samplings:

Butterhead Lettuce
Maturation: About 70 days

Butterhead lettuce is one of the more common lettuces and comes in several varieties including Bibb and Dark Green Boston. It produces loosely open heads of delicate but crisp leaves.

In the Garden
It is best to grow Butterhead lettuce from plants. Or sow them from seeds indoors, and set them in moist, well-drained, fertile soil as early as the ground can be worked, placing the plants 10 to 12 inches (25 to 30 cm) apart. Since it is relatively fast-growing, a second crop of Butterhead can be cultivated in midsummer. To harvest, pick leaves or cut the head at ground level, or carefully pull up head, roots and all.

Crisphead Lettuce
Maturation: About 90 days

Also known as Iceberg lettuce, this tight, brittle lettuce has gone out of fashion among serious cooks because the store-bought varieties (like other commercially grown produce) are often virtually tasteless. It is also difficult to grow at home since it is highly heat sensitive. Nevertheless, Iceberg lettuce is the crispest lettuce, so for those who prefer crunchiness in their salads, this remains the best choice. It is also the lettuce used in certain ethnic cuisines, such as Mexican and Chinese.

In the Garden
Start plants indoors (or buy them), and place them about 12 inches (30 cm) apart in moist, loamy, well-drained soil. Make sure the lettuce is shaded at least part of the day. Harvest when the center of the head (the most flavorful part) is hard. Cut off at ground level.

Leaf Lettuce
Maturation: About 50 days

Leaf lettuce is a good-looking, flavorful lettuce that comes in several varieties, including Black Seeded Simpson, Grand Rapids, and Red Salad Bowl. It is one of the more popular lettuces for the home gardener,

Leaf lettuce (far left) and Romaine lettuce (near left) growing in the garden.

because it grows quickly and easily, and is more heat-resistant than many other lettuce varieties.

In the Garden

Although you can start seeds indoors or buy plants, leaf lettuce grows quickly from seeds sown directly in the garden. Sow seeds as soon as soil is ready in spring, keep moist, and fertilize every 3 or 4 weeks to ensure quicker growth. Plant a second crop in late summer. To harvest, gather leaves when they are ready.

Romaine Lettuce
Maturation: About 75 days

Romaine lettuce is an upright lettuce with more oblong leaves than other lettuces.

Romaine is somewhat more difficult to grow than Butterhead or leaf lettuce, but its delicious flavor makes it well worth the effort. Caesar salad is the signature dish for Romaine lettuce.

In the Garden

Start seeds indoors or buy plants, and set the plants in the garden in early spring, about 10 to 12 inches (25 to 30 cm) apart. (Romaine can also be grown in winter in warmer climates.) To harvest, pick leaves or cut the entire head at ground level.

In the Kitchen

All lettuces are, of course, the basis of the tossed salad and the classic filler accompaniment to many sandwiches. However, lettuce can also be served sautéed in butter as a side dish, stuffed, and even baked.

79

Baked Lettuce, Hungarian Style

Makes 6 servings as a side dish

2 or 3 small heads of Bibb or Boston lettuce
2 cups dairy sour cream
2 large tomatoes, sliced
Salt to taste
2 tablespoons chopped fresh basil
¼ cup bread crumbs
4 tablespoons (½ stick) butter

Preheat oven to 350 degrees F (170° C). Generously grease (with butter) an 8-×8-inch (20-×20-cm) cake pan.

Blanch lettuce very quickly in boiling water, drain, and dry leaves on towel.

In the cake pan, spread about 4 tablespoons of the sour cream, then line the pan with the lettuce leaves. Top with a few tomato slices, add salt, and sprinkle with basil. Repeat the layers until all the ingredients have been used.

Sprinkle bread crumbs on top, dot with butter, and bake for about 10 minutes, or until the vegetables are warmed through and the top is golden brown. Serve warm.

© Michael Nelson/FPG International

Romaine lettuce is one of the most flavorful lettuce greens.

Simple Garden Salad with Parsley Vinaigrette

Serves 4

This is a basic green salad dressed with a basic French vinaigrette dressing; however, it can be altered in endless ways. Substitute radicchio, watercress, Boston lettuce, or any number of herb greens for the lettuces. Add or substitute basil, rosemary, thyme, tarragon, or any herb that suits your palate for the parsley. Finally, consider any combination of flavored vinegars (raspberry, for example) or oils (hazelnut oil is delicious). If you have a sweet tooth, honey adds a nice consistency to the vinaigrette. The only limitation is your own creativity!

4 to 6 cups fresh garden lettuces (Bibb, leaf, Romaine, Butterhead, etc.) carefully washed and torn into pieces
1 cup arugula, washed and torn into pieces
1 Belgian endive, sliced
1 clove garlic, peeled and minced
2 tablespoons minced fresh parsley
⅔ cup olive oil
3 tablespoons white wine vinegar
1 teaspoon grainy mustard
Salt to taste
Freshly ground black pepper to taste

Wash and dry the greens carefully and toss together in a bowl. Chill.

Whisk together the garlic, parsley, and olive oil. Add the vinegar, whisk; add the mustard and continue whisking until the dressing is smooth. Add salt and pepper.

Pour the dressing over the greens just before serving.

A simple garden salad incorporating a mélange of greens.

© Ralph B. Pleasant/FPG International

81

PEAS
Maturation: About 65 days

Probably because peas were one of the first vegetables to be commercially canned in the mid-nineteenth century, the vegetable brings to mind an unattractive gray-green mound of mush for many of us, and conjures up images of hotel dining rooms and Sunday dinners at Grandma's house. However, these canned varieties don't begin to compare with homegrown green peas. Peas grow on shrubs or vines and are hardy plants, and therefore can be cultivated in very early spring in northern climates and throughout the winter in the South. Varieties include Green Arrow, Little Marvel, and Maestro.

In recent years, podded peas or Snow peas and Snap peas—those consumed pod and all—have become popular, especially for use in Oriental dishes. Varieties include Sugar Snap and Sugar Daddy.

In the Garden
Plant pea seeds (all varieties) as soon as the soil is workable in fertile, sandy, well-drained soil. Peas need little fertilization. Plant seeds about 1 inch (2.5 cm) deep, and 2 inches (5 cm) apart. Put shrubby varieties in rows about 24 inches (60 cm) apart and vine varieties about 36 inches (90 cm) apart.

(Vining peas may need a trellis, pole, or stake.) Harvest green peas when the pods become swollen, but before the peas turn hard.

Harvest Snow peas when they are about 2 inches (5 cm) long, succulent but still flat. Pick Sugar Snap peas when their pods are round and pebbly, but before they turn yellow.

In the Kitchen
Green peas must be removed from the pods before they are cooked, which is somewhat tedious, but well worth the effort. Fresh peas are as sweet as candy. They are a marvelous accompaniment to meats, particularly roast chicken, and are a colorful and flavorful addition to soups, salads, and rice dishes. Pea soup is a classic dish and is so hearty that on cold winter days it can be served as a welcoming meal in itself. (Pea soup is usually made with dried peas. If you adore peas—and pea soup—it might be worthwhile to dry part of your crop for use during the winter months.)

Shelled peas can be canned, frozen, or dried with great success.

Sugar Snap peas and Snow Peas are prepared and eaten pod and all. Lightly blanched, either one makes a welcome and attractive addition to a crudite platter, and lightly steamed, both make an interesting side dish with roasted or grilled meats.

Fresh Peas with Mint

Makes 6 servings

3 pounds of peas in the pod
Salt to taste
3 tablespoons chopped mint
Freshly ground black pepper to taste
3 tablespoons chopped mint
3 tablespoons butter

Shell the peas. In a saucepan, bring water —enough to just cover the peas—to a boil. Add salt, pepper, half the mint, and the peas, and cook for about 15 minutes, or until the peas are tender. Spoon the peas into a warmed serving dish. In a small skillet, melt the butter and pour it over the peas. Sprinkle with the remaining mint.

© Jay Brenner/FPG International

Fresh steamed peas taste like candy.

PEPPERS
Maturation: About 60 to 80 days

There are basically two types of peppers, sweet peppers and hot peppers. Sweet peppers, which are usually bell shaped, come in several varieties (Bell Boy, California Wonder, Gypsy) and colors—green, yellow, and purple. Hot peppers, which are elongated cone shapes, also come in several varieties (Jalapa, Mexibell, Red Cherry Hot), and are most frequently—and best—grown in warmer climates.

In the Garden
Hot peppers should be started indoors and then transplanted outdoors after the last frost in rich, well-drained soil. (Seeds can be started outdoors if the growing season is very long.) Space the plants (which grow to about 2 feet [60 cm] in height), about 2 feet (60 cm) apart in rows about 3 feet (90 cm) apart. Fertilize at planting time. Harvest when peppers turn red.

Sweet peppers are generally cultivated using the same methods as hot peppers, although they will mature somewhat more quickly. Most people harvest peppers when they are firm and green, but you can wait until they turn red. Red peppers are somewhat sweeter than green peppers. Most plants will produce more fruits after the first harvest.

In the Kitchen
Peppers are popular culinary vegetables and in recent years, cooks have come to appreciate the uses of sweet yellow peppers and sweet red peppers. Peppers can be served raw in salads or cooked, usually stuffed, as a main course or appetizer.

Hot peppers are normally associated with Mexican and other cuisines where the climate is hot. Hot dips made of jalapeño peppers are popular in the American Southwest, and chilis of all kinds are the signature food of the chili pepper.

A sliced green pepper fresh from the garden.

Nina's Sausage and Peppers Sauté

Makes 6 servings

This quick, colorful, and delicious one-dish meal comes compliments of my friend, Nina, whose Italian grandmother used to serve a similar dish. Serve with warm garlic bread and a light, red Italian wine.

2 tablespoons olive oil
1/2 pound sweet Italian sausage
1/2 pound hot Italian sausage
2 hot peppers, minced
1 large yellow onion, minced
2 cloves garlic, peeled and minced
6 plum tomatoes, seeded and chopped
2 teaspoons tomato paste
2 green peppers, seeded and chopped
2 sweet red peppers, seeded and chopped
2 teaspoons fresh oregano
2 teaspoons fresh marjoram
1 bay leaf
Salt to taste
Freshly ground black pepper to taste
1/2 cup freshly grated Parmesan cheese

In a large skillet, heat the olive oil. Add the sausages and sauté until browned. When cooked, slice into rings, and set aside.

Remove all but 4 tablespoons of fat from the skillet. Add the hot peppers, onion, and garlic, and sauté until browned. Add the tomatoes, tomato paste, green and red peppers, oregano, marjoram, bay leaf, salt, and pepper. Cover the skillet, and simmer for about 20 minutes until the sauce has thickened.

Add the sausages and simmer for 5 minutes more. Remove the bay leaf and correct the seasonings. Sprinkle with the Parmesan cheese and serve.

© Bill Margerin/FPG International

Red, green, and yellow peppers ready to be incorporated into a sausage and pepper sauté.

POTATOES

Maturation: About 110 days

Potatoes, whether they are white baking potatoes or red (or brown) boiling potatoes, are cultivated in much the same way. Like onions, carrots, and other root vegetables, they do not grow well in clay soil. And, since they are so inexpensive to buy, many home gardeners don't bother planting potatoes. However, second only to a feast of freshly picked, steamed corn-on-the-cob, an autumn luncheon of new potatoes gathered from the field, boiled with fresh dill or parsley and laden with butter, is one of life's little wonders.

In the Garden

Potatoes of all varieties should be grown from purchased tubers called seed potatoes, which are required to be free of disease. Plant seed potatoes in early spring, 4 to 6 weeks before the last frost. Plant them about 4 inches (10 cm) deep, 12 inches (30 cm) apart in sandy, well-drained soil. Fertilize at planting time, and water sparingly. (Overwatering can cause rotting.) When the

© Michael Grand

plants get to be about 6 inches (15 cm) high, pile soil over them to keep out the light, which tends to turn the potatoes green and bitter. Repeat when the tops get to be about 15 to 18 inches (38 to 45 cm) high. The tubers are ready to harvest when the plant flowers and dies back. To harvest, carefully dig down and pull out the potatoes.

A humble wooden bowl filled with unassuming potatoes—including Idaho white potatoes, red potatoes, and sweet potatoes.

Potatoes Baked
with Garlic and Cheese

Makes 6 servings

6 large baking potatoes, peeled
2 large cloves garlic, peeled and minced
Salt to taste
Freshly ground black pepper to taste
2 cups heavy cream
½ cup grated Swiss cheese

Preheat oven to 300 degrees F (149° C).

Butter a 9-×9-inch (23-×23- cm) baking dish. Slice two of the potatoes thinly and spread the slices in the dish. Sprinkle with half the garlic and the salt and pepper. Pour in cream to cover. Repeat two more times until all the ingredients have been used (except for the cheese).

Bake the potatoes for 1½ hours. Sprinkle the cheese on top, then bake for another 30 minutes. Serve warm.

© Michael Skott

Potatoes baked with garlic and cheese are incredibly rich and equally irresistible.

RHUBARB
Maturation: 2 to 3 years

Rhubarb is sweet, and combines well with strawberries. It looks something like celery with tall stalks that are a pinkish red and large (poisonous) leaves. It is not an easy plant to cultivate, but people who particularly prize rhubarb (and there are a lot of them) find it worth the effort.

In the Garden
Rhubarb is a perennial plant and grows best where summers are warm (and days are long), and winters are cold. It is easiest to buy plants (or take divisions). Set the plants in rich, well-drained soil, about 4 feet (120 cm) apart. Rhubarb should not be harvested for at least 2 years and often 3 years, and then stalks are at their best in spring or early summer.

In the Kitchen
Stewed (or steamed) rhubarb and rhubarb pie are two desserts that inspire many gourmands. Since it is a springtime plant, it is often combined with strawberries (their flavors blend well together, too) and strawberry-rhubarb pie is considered a delicacy, especially in New England.

Rhubarb freezes well, and can be used to make preserves and jams.

Simple Spicy Rhubarb

Makes 4 servings

1 pound rhubarb stalks
½ cup sugar
¼ cup light brown sugar
¼ cup very hot water
2 tablespoons unsalted butter
Ground cinnamon to taste
Ground nutmeg to taste

Wash the rhubarb and slice it into 1-inch (2.5-cm) pieces. Place it in the top of a double boiler, over simmering water, and steam for 30 minutes, or until tender.

Dissolve the sugars in very hot water. Pour the sugar mixture over the rhubarb and steam for 5 minutes longer. Place the steamed rhubarb in a serving dish, dot with butter, and sprinkle with cinnamon and nutmeg to suit your taste. Serve warm.

Opposite: Rhubarb is as attractive in the garden as it is on the table.

© Steven Mark Needham/Envision

*A creamy spinach dip, perfect
for serving with vegetable
crudites.*

SPINACH

Maturation: About 50 days

Perhaps more jokes have been told about spinach than any other vegetable. From it, Popeye got his power and repeatedly won the heart of his sweetheart, Olive Oyl. It is known among small children as the most hated vegetable. But for those in the know (adults), spinach is a tasty and nutritious vegetable, easy to grow, and redolent with ideas for the creative cook.

In the Garden
Spinach grows best in cooler climates (or in the winter in the South). Plant seeds in moist, well-drained, alkaline soil in early spring. (A second crop can be cultivated in late summer.) Sow seeds about ½ inch (1 cm) deep, 2 to 4 inches (5 to 10 cm) apart, in rows about 18 inches (45 cm) apart. To harvest, cut its dark green leaves when they are about 6 or 8 inches (15 or 20 cm) long, but before the plant flowers, or cut the head completely at ground level.

In the Kitchen
Spinach, like other leafy vegetables, is excellent served raw in salads or cooked as a side dish with almost any grilled meat. It can be added to soups or can serve as the basis for a savory shav. Spinach freezes well, either chopped or with leaves left whole.

Spinach Shav

Makes 6 servings

8 or 10 spinach leaves, washed thoroughly and
  chopped into bite-sized pieces
2 cups water
1 teaspoon salt
Freshly ground black pepper to taste
Juice of 1 lemon
2 cups dairy sour cream
¼ teaspoon paprika
2 cucumbers, washed, peeled, seeded, and chopped

Place the spinach, water, salt, and pepper
in a medium-sized saucepan, bring to a
boil, and simmer for 10 minutes. Remove
from the heat, stir in the lemon juice, cool
slightly, then chill.

Just before serving, stir in the sour cream,
paprika, and cucumber. Serve cold.

**Spinach is a beautiful garden
vegetable—as easy to cultivate
as it is to prepare.**

91

Spinach Omelette

Makes 2 servings

Filling:

1 small white onion, minced
1 tablespoon butter
½ cup cooked spinach, drained and dried
3 tablespoons heavy cream
¼ teaspoon nutmeg
Salt and freshly ground black pepper to taste

3 eggs, at room temperature
3 tablespoons milk
2 tablespoons butter

To make the filling, sauté the onion in the 1 tablespoon butter in a small pan. Remove from the heat and add the spinach, heavy cream, nutmeg, salt, and pepper. Set aside.

Break the eggs in a bowl and whisk until they are about twice their original volume. Stir in the milk.

Melt the butter in a 10-inch (25-cm) skillet over medium-high heat and cook until it bubbles. Add the eggs, but do not stir them. When the eggs begin to firm up, top with the spinach mixture.

Preheat the broiler.

Hold the skillet above the heat source on the stove, tilting it from side to side until the edges begin to brown slightly. Pass the pan under the broiler for a few seconds, just long enough to cook the top slightly.

Remove the pan from the broiler. Fold the omelette in half and slide it out of the pan. Serve immediately.

Basic fixings for a spinach omelette.

SQUASH, WINTER
Maturation: About 75 to 90 days

Acorn squash (yellow or dark green acorn-shaped, ribbed squashes), spaghetti squash (yellow-white, smooth-skinned squashes), and butternut squash (large, bell-shaped, pale yellow squashes) are referred to as winter squashes because they can be stored, like onions and potatoes, in a dry, cool place for many months. All winter squashes grow on vines that usually grow to about 12 inches (30 cm) high and several feet (1 m) long.

The pumpkin is a close kin to winter squash. Pumpkins come in two species: Cucurbita pepo that produces the small pumpkins normally used for pumpkin pies and jack-o-lanterns; and Cucurbita maxima that produces those mammoth pumpkins you often see proudly displayed at harvest time in garden centers. For the average home gardener, it is probably wise to stick with a few plants of the smaller species. (Some farmers plant their pumpkins in among their corn plants; the two plants seem to grow well together.)

In the Garden
Because winter squashes (including pumpkins, which take as long as 120 days to mature) require a long growing season, seeds should be started indoors in early spring or plants should be purchased. Since squash plants do not transplant well, the plants should be started in peat pots and the pots planted in the garden in late spring about 3 feet (90 cm) apart. Squashes grow best in rich, loamy soil. Harvest all squashes as soon as the skin turns hard; leave a bit of stem on the squash when you pick it since a bruised squash will rot.

In the Kitchen
It is my understanding that a love for cooked squash is an acquired taste, but since I love squash in many of its incarnations (baked, in pies, etc.) I have trouble believing it. It is a colorful vegetable—the meat is usually a warm shade of orange—and is both naturally sweet and often prepared with sugar and cinnamon, making it a beautiful and flavorful accompaniment to roasts (beef, lamb, pork, or chicken) and even strong-flavored fish like bluefish.

Because squashes are naturally sweet, they are often used in baked goods such as cakes, cookies, custards, and, especially, pies. Pumpkin pie is a classic autumnal dessert, but both acorn squash and butternut squash make delicious pie fillings.

Winter squash and pumpkin can be canned by the pressured method. They can also be frozen. In both cases, they should be precooked and canned or frozen as puree.

Mom's Butternut Squash Pie

Makes one 9-inch (23-cm) pie

My mother never seems to have enough time on Thanksgiving eve to create a perfect pie crust, so she buys the frozen kind—most of which are delicious—and no one seems to mind. I've adopted her habit, I'm afraid, and I don't mind passing on the notion.

1 large butternut squash
3 eggs, beaten
½ cup heavy cream
½ cup light brown sugar
1 teaspoon cinnamon
½ teaspoon nutmeg
½ teaspoon ginger
½ teaspoon salt
One 9-inch (23- cm) store-bought frozen pie shell

Preheat oven to 350 degrees F (177° C).

Cut the squash into chunks and boil or steam them until the meat is soft. Peel off the skin and place the squash "meat" into a large mixing bowl. Add the eggs, cream, brown sugar, cinnamon, nutmeg, ginger, and salt, and beat with an electric mixer until the puree is well blended. Pour squash mixture into the pie shell, and bake for about 50 minutes, or until the custard sets. Serve warm or cool.

Various squashes, including butternut squashes, pumpkins, and gourds.

© Derek Fell

*"Table Ace" acorn squash
ready to be harvested.*

Baked Acorn Squash

Makes 6 servings

This is a simple and delicious way to cook acorn squash and to serve it with roasts or grilled meats. Serve the vegetable in its skin as a side dish.

3 firm acorn squashes
6 tablespoons (¾ stick) butter
3 tablespoons dark brown sugar
3 teaspoons cinnamon

Preheat oven to 350 degrees F (177° C). Wash the squashes, cut them in half, remove seeds and fibers, and place on a baking sheet. Put a tablespoon of butter into the center of each squash, then sprinkle each with brown sugar and cinnamon. Cover each squash with tin foil and bake for 40 to 45 minutes until the squash is soft. Serve hot.

A ripe and beautiful Pattypan, or Yellow, squash.

SQUASH, SUMMER
Maturation: About 50 days

Summer squashes are tender squashes that are harvested and eaten during the summer (before the skin becomes hard). They include crookneck squash (a yellow, curved-neck variety that has either a warty skin or a smooth skin), straight neck squash (a yellow, smooth-skinned squash with a straight neck), zucchini squash (a small green squash with a straight neck and a large, yellow flower), and scallop squash (a round, scallop-shaped squash that can be yellow, or light or dark green).

In the Garden
All summer squashes like rich, well-drained soil and don't require extensive sunlight. Sow seeds or set plants in the garden after the last chance of frost has passed. Sow seeds about ½ inch (1 cm) deep and 18 inches (45 cm) apart in rows about 4 feet (120 cm) apart. Fertilize at planting time and once again in midsummer. Water as the soil dries out.

Harvest summer squash when it is about 5 inches (13 cm) long and 2 inches (5 cm) wide, and the skin is still tender and can be pricked with a fingernail. Summer squash tends to grow quickly (within 50 days) and must be checked almost daily for ripe fruits. Zucchini squash also produces large yellow flowers that are edible.

Many beginning gardeners tend to over-plant summer squash and are overwhelmed by midsummer. Consider how much squash you will truly be able to use and, as a rule-of-thumb, plant on the conservative side.

In the Kitchen
In recent years, North Americans have finally come to appreciate the delectable flavor of summer squash served raw as a crudite or in salads. The sweet meaty flesh, when served fresh and crisp, is ideal as a dipper or a crunchy salad component.

Perhaps because summer squash is so prolific and easy to grow, recipes for squash—particularly zucchini—abound. It can be chopped and used in omelettes or quiches, baked into breads, cakes, and pancakes, and cooked in innumerable ways and with many other vegetables for an interesting and always-compatible side dish.

Summer squash is also an easy vegetable to can using the pressure cooking method. In addition, squash freezes well. Thus, choices for dealing with a huge crop of summer squash are endless. And we have not even discussed giving away a pound or two to neighbors and friends.

Cream of Zucchini Soup with Curry

Makes 4 servings

Served hot or cold, this is a refreshing summer soup, so hearty it can almost be served as a luncheon main course.

1 pound fresh zucchini (about 6 young zucchini)
2 tablespoons butter
2 tablespoons minced shallots
2 cloves garlic, peeled and minced
1 teaspoon curry powder
½ teaspoon salt
Freshly ground black pepper to taste
½ cup water
2 cups half-and-half

Wash, trim, and thinly slice the zucchini. Put the zucchini in a saucepan with the butter, shallots, garlic, curry powder, salt, and pepper, and cook over low heat for about 5 minutes, shaking the pan frequently, until the vegetables are softened.

Add the water and simmer for 10 minutes, stirring occasionally. Puree the vegetables in a blender or in a food processor. Return the vegetables to the saucepan and add the half-and-half. Reheat and serve hot, or chill and serve cold.

Note: After pureeing, the cooked vegetables can be frozen. When you wish to serve the soup, simply defrost the vegetables, add the half-and-half, heat, and serve.

© Derek Fell

The ubiquitous zucchini growing in the garden.

Glenn David Smith

Zucchini bread has a natural sweetness that is unmistakable.

Buddy's All-Ohio Zucchini Bread

Makes 1 loaf

1 cup sifted all-purpose flour
1 cup unsifted stone-ground whole wheat flour
½ teaspoon salt
1 teaspoon baking soda
8 tablespoons (1 stick) butter
1 cup sugar
1 tablespoon grated orange rind
2 tablespoons orange juice
3 eggs
2 cups peeled and chopped zucchini
½ cup chopped walnuts

Preheat oven to 325 degrees F (167°C). Grease a 9- × 5- × 3-inch (23- × 13- × 8-cm) loaf pan.

Sift flours, salt, and baking soda together and set aside. In a bowl, cream the butter and sugar together until light and fluffy. Add the orange rind and orange juice, and blend; then add the eggs one at a time, beating well after each additional egg. Add the zucchini and mix well. Blend in the nuts.

Put the dough in the loaf pan and bake for 1 hour or until cake tester inserted in center comes out clean. Turn out on a wire rack and cool before slicing.

99

STRAWBERRIES
Maturation: About 8 to 14 months

Cultivated strawberries are low-to-the-ground perennial plants that have little spiky leaves, pretty white flowers, and the world's most delicious fruit.

In the Garden
Strawberries grow close to the ground and send out "runners" that form new plants at their nodules. Set strawberry plants (it is best to buy plants) in the ground in early spring in the North (they will produce fruit the following summer) or in the fall in the South (they will produce fruit the following spring). Set the plants in rich light soil (sandy soil is best) that is well drained about 2 feet (60 cm) apart in rows 6 feet (180 cm) apart. Fertilize in spring and summer and mulch to retain moisture. Pick berries as soon as they are red and ripe.

In the Kitchen
No one needs to be instructed how to prepare and eat a strawberry: Most of the time you pluck it from the plant and pop it in your mouth. For the more civilized, Strawberries and Cream (or ice cream) is the second-best method of preparing this fruit.

Strawberry jams, preserves, and sauces are easily made and serve as delectable treats long after the season has passed. Strawberries also can be frozen.

© Derek Fell

Strawberries—the world's most delicious fruit.

Strawberries and Cream

Makes 4 servings

Wild strawberries are smaller and have a slightly less-sweet flavor than the larger cultivated varieties, but are a special treat, too. Try to serve all the varieties of strawberries within hours of picking.

4 cups freshly picked strawberries
2 cups heavy cream
Sprigs of fresh spearmint

Pick over the berries, wash thoroughly in cool water, divide evenly among four serving dishes, and keep refrigerated until serving time. Garnish each dish with a sprig of spearmint. Pass a pitcher of heavy cream.

Note: Strawberries can also be served with crème fraîche or with a dash of Grand Marnier.

© Guy Powers/Envision

Strawberries topped with custard, a classic dessert.

101

*The almost comical sunflower
produces nutritious seeds.*

SUNFLOWER
Maturation: About 120 days

Cultivated for seeds *(Helianthus annuus)* or for their delicious tubers *(Helianthus tuberosus),* sunflowers are a dramatic and interesting addition to any garden. (The leaves and flower buds also can be added to certain dishes.) Sunflowers are native to North America and were originally cultivated by the American Indians.

In the Garden
Sunflowers need full sun and well-drained loamy soil. Sow seeds in spring, then transplant to 12 to 18 inches (30 to 45 cm) apart. To harvest, pick leaves and flower buds as required. To collect the seeds, cut the flower heads and hang upside down until the seeds fall, or cover the head with a paper bag. Dig up tuberous roots in autumn. To preserve, dry seeds and store tubers in a cool place.

In the Kitchen
Sunflower seeds are nutritious—for birds as well as humans. Eat the seeds raw or roasted in their shells. Sprouted seeds are delicious in salads or sandwiches. Raw flower buds can also be added to salads.

The tuberous roots of one variety of sunflower are known as Jerusalem artichokes. They can be cooked and served as a vegetable, or grated and added to salads.

Jerusalem Artichokes in Cream

Makes 4 servings

Jerusalem artichokes are the tuberous roots
of the North American sunflower. They are
not true artichokes, but have a similar flavor
to the well-known French artichoke. This
recipe is especially delicious served as an
accompaniment to roasted veal, pork, or
roast beef.

1 pound Jerusalem artichokes
8 tablespoons (1 stick) butter
1 cup heavy cream
1 tablespoon chopped chervil

   Peel the Jerusalem artichokes, and cut
into quarters or trim to egg shapes. Blanch
for 5 minutes in boiling water, then drain.
   Melt the butter, add the blanched artichokes, and simmer for about 30 minutes,
or until tender. Stir in the heavy cream and
simmer for 10 minutes. Spoon onto a
warmed serving platter and sprinkle with
the chervil.

© Derek Fell

The tubers from **Helianthus**
tuberosus, *a variety of*
sunflower, are known as
Jerusalem artichokes.

TOMATOES
Maturation: 60–90 days

Tomatoes are one of the most popular plants grown in a home vegetable garden. Not even the most expensive commercially grown tomato can compare to the delightful homegrown tomato, which fairly bursts with flavor. In general, tomatoes fall into two groups—determinate tomatoes and indeterminate tomatoes.

Determinate tomatoes are bushy plants that stop growing when they reach maturity and the fruit ripens at the same time. (The plants bear only one crop.) Indeterminate tomatoes are vines that grow, flower, and produce fruit until the plants are killed by frost. Determinate tomatoes include plum tomatoes and other varieties best used for canning, sauces, and juice. Indeterminate tomatoes are the delectable fruits we love eating plucked from the vine, sliced, or in salads.

Cherry tomatoes, or small tomatoes about an inch (2.5 cm) in diameter, grow on vines or on dwarf plants. Like their larger cousins, they can be either determinate or indeterminate. Determinate cherry tomatoes are very versatile plants that will also grow well in containers, or hanging baskets —indoors or out.

In the Garden
Determinate and indeterminate tomatoes are cultivated in much the same way. In most climates, it is best to start plants indoors (or buy them), and then set the plants in the garden after any danger of frost has passed, in soil that is rich, evenly moist, slightly acid, and well drained.

Place determinate tomatoes about 2 feet (60 cm) apart. Fertilize at planting time, apply mulch, and keep moist. As the fruit ripens, decrease the watering so that the fruit is meatier and more flavorful.

Indeterminate tomatoes can be left growing on the ground, but the fruit will be smaller and ripen more slowly than if the vines are staked. If indeterminate vines are staked, they should be pruned back to one stem and grown on a stake or trellis 18 to 24 inches (45 to 60 cm) apart. Staked plants will produce larger fruit and will ripen faster.

Pick all tomatoes as soon as they ripen. In late fall, pick green tomatoes before the frost and let them ripen inside in a warm sunny place.

In the Kitchen
In many of the world's cuisines—Hispanic, Italian, Indian, French, and American— tomatoes are considered a kitchen staple. They are delicious raw, freshly plucked from the vine, and sliced and dressed with an herb vinaigrette; but are equally tasty stewed, stuffed, baked, or mixed into stews, sauces, ketchups, and juices. The tomato is one of the world's most versatile foods.

© Derek Fell

Various varieties of tomatoes including red, yellow, and cherry tomatoes.

If you produce a bumper crop of tomatoes, plan to can several pounds for use during the winter months. Tomatoes do not freeze well fresh from the garden, but tomato sauces and soups freeze beautifully. Consider making your favorite Italian tomato sauce with end-of-the-season fruits and freezing it for cold autumn nights.

Katherine's Old-Fashioned Cream of Tomato Soup

Makes 6 cups

My great-aunt Katherine taught English literature at Case Western Reserve University in Ohio, but during the summer months, she retired to her family home in upstate New York and spent many hours tending her garden. As a child, I would often visit her during the last week of my summer vacation and, invariably, she would make the following tomato soup from beautiful tomatoes picked fresh from her garden.

2 cups fresh tomatoes, peeled and chopped
½ cup chopped celery
¼ cup chopped onion
1 tablespoon sugar
8 tablespoons (1 stick) butter
½ cup all-purpose flour
4 cups heavy cream
Salt and freshly ground black pepper to taste
¼ cup chopped fresh tarragon

In a saucepan, place the tomatoes, celery, onion, and sugar, and simmer for about 15 minutes until the vegetables are softened.

In another saucepan, melt the butter, then add the flour and blend, over low heat, for 3 or 4 minutes until smooth. Slowly add the cream, stirring constantly with a

wooden spoon or whisk, for about 15 minutes until the roux is thick and smooth. Add the sauce to the tomato stock. Blend thoroughly, then add the salt and pepper.

Pour the soup into bowls and garnish with the chopped tarragon. Serve warm.

Note: This is a very thick, hearty soup. If you wish a thinner variation, substitute milk for half the cream. Also, this soup is equally delicious garnished with fresh chives or basil, or served cold, garnished with parsley or chives.

Cream of tomato soup, seasoned with basil.

106

Simple Tomato Sauce

Makes about 4 cups

This recipe makes a thick, rustic sauce that is ideal served over spaghetti or any filled pastas.

3 tablespoons olive oil
3 tablespoons butter
1 large onion, finely chopped
3 celery ribs, finely chopped
1 carrot, chopped
1 green pepper, finely chopped
1 clove garlic, minced
6 large plum tomatoes, chopped
1 tablespoon chopped basil
1 tablespoon chopped tarragon
1 teaspoon salt
Freshly ground black pepper to taste

In a large skillet, heat the olive oil and butter together, then add the onion, celery, carrot, green pepper, and garlic, and sauté until the vegetables begin to soften, about 5 minutes. Add the tomatoes, basil, tarragon, salt, and pepper, and simmer over low heat for about 1 hour, until the sauce thickens. Adjust the seasonings, and serve hot.

© Ralph Chandler/FPG International

Note: This sauce freezes well. Depending upon your taste, 2 cups of sauce is sufficient for a pound of pasta (spaghetti, fettuccine, etc.) that usually serves four. Consider serving half the sauce as you cook it, and freezing the other half.

A rustic tomato sauce seasoned with herbs is perfect over pasta.

Simple Fresh Tomato Salad

Makes 4 servings

Few foods are as delicious as tomatoes served just hours after being picked from the vine. They are so sweet and flavorful, they require little (or no) dressing.

2 or 3 large tomatoes
¼ cup small fresh basil leaves
Salt to taste
Freshly ground black pepper to taste
Virgin olive oil to taste

   Slice the tomatoes into thick slices and arrange them on a platter. Scatter the basil leaves over the tomatoes, sprinkle with salt, pepper, and a few dribbles of olive oil.

Note: Good mozzarella cheese (Buffalo or smoked) is a delicious complement to a fresh tomato salad. For this recipe, buy about ½ pound (.23 kg) of cheese, thinly slice it, and layer between the tomato slices.

Tomatoes are best eaten fresh from the vine or with a light herb-and-oil dressing.

Roasted Brook Trout with Tomato, Zucchini, and Basil

Makes 4 servings

This recipe was created by Chef Waldy Malouf of New York's chic Hudson River Club at the World Trade Center. It can also be served as an appetizer, for up to 8.

½ cup extra-virgin olive oil
2 zucchini, sliced
4 large, very ripe tomatoes, peeled and sliced
2 handfuls of fresh basil, finely shredded
4 shallots, thinly sliced
Coarse salt and freshly ground black pepper to
*   taste*
Juice of 1 lemon
¼ cup all-purpose flour
Four 12-to-14-ounce fresh brook trout, cleaned,
*   eviscerated, and gills removed*
½ cup dry white wine

Preheat oven to 450 degrees F (232°C).

Line a shallow 8- x 12-inch (20- x 30- cm) baking dish with a third of the olive oil. In an alternating pattern, layer the zucchini and the tomato rounds until the vegetables line the entire pan. Sprinkle the basil and the shallots evenly over the tomatoes and zucchini. Add the salt and pepper and dribble the lemon juice over all the vegetables.

Lightly flour the cleaned trout, shaking off the excess flour. Place the trout on top

© Anita Sabarese

of the vegetables and drizzle the remaining olive oil and the wine over the trout.

Roast in the oven, uncovered, for 20 minutes.

Remove the trout to a warm platter and debone to produce eight fillets. Cover and keep warm.

With a spatula, transfer the layered vegetables to the serving plates. Place the trout fillets over the vegetables.

Pour the liquid from the roasting pan into a small saucepan and bring it to a boil. Adjust the seasonings if necessary and pour it over each fillet.

Serve immediately.

Basil adds special flavor to any dish.

110

Chapter 5

A FEW CULINARY HERBS AND EDIBLE FLOWERS

Opposite: Chives, rosemary, basil, and nasturtiums grown in the herb garden will complement many dishes made from your own vegetables. Right: A sprig of rosemary, tarragon, and sage, tied with twine, ready for drying.

© Amy Reichman/Envision

The following is a list of a few common herbs often found in a workable kitchen herb garden, together with growing tips and culinary suggestions. These herbs are easy to plant among or beside your vegetables in the garden. Since many of the herbs are perennials while most of the vegetables are annuals, you should probably consider creating a separate bed for your herbs—if you have not done so already. On the other hand, consider making a border for your vegetable garden out of nasturtium plants or some variety of rosemary. Both will create a very pretty hedge and also help to keep certain garden pests at bay.

111

BASIL
Annual
Height: 15 to 18 inches (38 to 46 cm)

Basil is one of the most esteemed culinary herbs. Because of its warm, spicy flavor, it has been used for thousands of years. Along with oregano, basil is almost essential to any Italian dish, especially those containing tomatoes. (Pesto made with basil leaves, is, of course, a classic Italian sauce.) There are many varieties of basil, some with a marvelous lemony fragrance.

In the Garden
Basil grows best in warm climates, and requires a sunny, warm spot that is protected from wind, frost, or excessive sun that might scorch the leaves. Sow basil in pots or after the last frost. Plant it in well-drained, moist soil, then thin or transplant to 8 inches (20 cm) apart. To harvest, pick leaves when young. To preserve, freeze or dry leaves or store whole leaves in olive oil.

In the Kitchen
Basil leaves are very delicate, so when preparing, tear rather than chop the leaves, and add them in cooked dishes at the last minute. Basil leaves are also delicious sprinkled over salads and infused in vinegars and oils, particularly olive oil.

BAY
Shrub or Evergreen Tree
Height: 6 to 12 feet (180 to 360 cm)

Bay is a large shrub or tree that can be pruned into elegant shapes. The leaves have a pungent aroma. It can be grown in a container and taken inside in winter.

In the Garden
A bay laurel tree needs full sun, protection from winds, and rich, moist, well-drained soil. To propagate, plant cuttings in a heated propagator with high humidity, then transplant to a frost-free area for the first two years. (Bay laurel is not easy to propagate, so it may be easier to buy a plant and transplant to your garden.) During the summer, keep plants pruned for best growth. Pick leaves anytime; and dry leaves to preserve them for cooking.

In the Kitchen
Bay is one of the classic flavors found in Italian and French cuisine and is part of a traditional *bouquet garni*. Bay leaves are often added whole to stews, soups, sauces, marinades, stuffings, and pâtés, but since the bay leaves are coarse and not easily digestible, they should always be removed before a dish is served.

Chives

Hardy perennial
Height: 12 to 24 inches (30 to 60 cm)

Chives are members of the onion family.
The chives most associated with culinary
endeavors include ordinary chives *(A.
schoenoprasum)* with its beautiful pink
flowers, and Chinese chives *(A. tuberosum).*

In the Garden

Chives are hardy and easy to grow. Plant
chives in a sunny area in rich moist soil.
Sow seeds in spring, or divide bulbs in
autumn or spring, and enrich the soil annu-
ally. During the growing season, thin or
transplant plants to 9 inches (23 cm) apart
and water when dry. To increase the flavor
of the leaves and stems, remove the flowers.
To harvest, cut leaves, leaving 2 inches
(5 cm) for regrowth, and pick flowers as
they open.

To preserve, freeze or dry chive leaves
and stems. The leaves will stay fresh for up
to a week if refrigerated in plastic.

In the Kitchen

Chive leaves, chopped, are used universally
as a garnish for soups and sauces. The
flowers are very tasty, and can be used as a
lovely garnish or as a flavoring in vinegar.

Chives in full bloom.

113

MARJORAM
Perennial
Height: 6 to 20 inches (15 to 50 cm)

Marjoram, or sweet marjoram, is part of the oregano family. It has a sweet scent and a spicy flavor, long associated with many Mediterranean cuisines.

In the Garden
Marjoram should be planted in full sun with some shade, in well-drained, dry, alkaline soil. Marjoram tends to have a stronger flavor when grown in rich soil. Sow seeds indoors in spring, and plant seedlings about 8 inches (20 cm) apart, then fertilize. Divide plants in spring or autumn; take root or stem cuttings from late spring to midsummer. Thin out or transplant seedlings to 12 to 18 inches (30 to 45 cm) apart, and prune back the plants before they die. To harvest, pick young leaves anytime; to preserve, freeze or dry leaves.

In the Kitchen
Sweet marjoram leaves have a distinctive sweet-and-spicy flavor. Use them to make an aromatic tea or add them to salads. Use the leaves to flavor Italian foods, vegetables, stuffings, and fish, poultry, and meat dishes. Sweet marjoram is also used in Greek, Moroccan, and other Mediterranean cuisines.

MINTS
Hardy perennial
Height: 1½ inches to 3 feet (4 cm to 90 cm)

Traditionally a symbol of hospitality, mint comes in over 600 varieties and is one of the most popular herbs for the culinary garden. (For culinary uses, consider spearmint, crinkle-leaved black peppermint, apple-mint, English pennyroyal, or lemon mint.) It is an attractive plant for the garden, and an extremely useful and flavorful plant in the kitchen.

In the Garden
Mints can grow in sun or partial shade and require moist, well-drained, nutrient-rich, alkaline soil. To propagate, take root or stem cuttings or divide in spring and autumn, or sow seeds in spring. Thin or transplant to 9 to 12 inches (23 to 30 cm) apart, and remove all flowering stems to avoid cross-pollination between species, which is common with mints. Mint often grows best in pots because the roots grow wildly and tend to invade other plants. To harvest, pick leaves just before flowering. To preserve, dry or freeze the leaves, or infuse them in oil or vinegar.

In the Kitchen
The mints are remarkably versatile herbs. Spearmint and peppermint make invigorating teas and are delicious in sauces, vinegars,

Mint, including English pennyroyal (far left) and lemon mint (near left), adds a fresh flavor to many recipes.

and syrups. They are also delicious crystallized in sugar and used for decoration on cakes, cookies, and other confectioneries.

Although mint is normally associated with sweet flavors, the leaves add a fresh flavor to vegetables, potatoes, rice, stuffings, and even certain stews and soups. Many Middle Eastern and Mediterranean cuisines sprinkle mint over grilled meats and other savory dishes for a surprising flavor. Tabouli, the popular Middle Eastern salad, is flavored with mint.

115

NASTURTIUM
Annual
Height: About 12 inches (30 cm)

Nasturtiums are grown both as flowers and as herbs. They come in various colors—red, orange, and yellow—have rounded leaves, and make a bright addition to the garden. The peppery flavored flowers, buds, and leaves add a piquant taste to salads.

In the Garden
Nasturtiums require sunny placement and light, somewhat dry, well-drained soil. Sow seeds in spring after the last frost, about 8 to 12 inches (20 to 30 cm) apart. To harvest, pick stems at ground level, and use the leaves, buds, or flowers while fresh.

In the Kitchen
Nasturtium adds a zesty, peppery flavor to salads, fruit dishes, egg dishes, pasta dishes, and light stews, sauces, and soups. The flowers and leaves also make attractive garnishes.

OREGANO
Perennial
Height: 8 to 24 inches (20 to 60 cm)

Oregano comes in a number of varieties—including Italian oregano and Greek oregano, which is very flavorful. It is often included in a bouquet garni, especially for dishes native to southern France and other Mediterranean cultures. It is one of the most important culinary herbs.

In the Garden
Oregano grows best in full sun in light, well-drained, alkaline soil. To propagate, sow seeds in spring and plant seedlings about 12 inches (30 cm) apart in late spring. Divide plants in spring, or take stem cuttings. To harvest, cut leaves anytime. To preserve, hang stems upside down to dry, and then separate leaves.

In the Kitchen
Oregano has distinctive peppery or savory flavored leaves. The leaves can be chopped and blended with spicy foods such as pizza, egg, and cheese dishes, grilled meats, and spicy sauces and stews. Oregano combines well with certain other herbs—like garlic—and makes a marvelous garlic/oregano butter sauce.

Parsley

Hardy biennial
Height: 12 to 18 inches (30 to 45 cm)

Like several other popular culinary herbs, parsley boasts many varieties, but curled parsley and Italian parsley are those most commonly associated with cooking. All parsleys are rich in vitamins, minerals, and chlorophyll (which serves to cleanse the digestive system), and are attractive as a garnishing herb. Also, parsley is an ingredient in a classic bouquet garni.

In the Garden

Parsley requires full sun or light shade and rich, moist soil. If grown from seed, sow from spring to late summer; however, parsley is slow to germinate so purchased plants often prove more productive. Thin or transplant to 9 to 12 inches (23 to 30 cm) apart. Protect in cold weather or take indoors where it flourishes.

To harvest, cut leaves with scissors. (They are best during the first year.) Dig up roots

© Derek Fell

Plain leaf parsley will thrive equally well out-of-doors or inside on the kitchen windowsill.

in autumn of second year. Dry or freeze leaves.

In the Kitchen

Add parsley leaves raw to salads. When cooking, chop and add at the last minute to preserve the flavor. Parsley mingles well with egg dishes, vegetable dishes, and particularly with potatoes, soups, stews, sauces, and light fish dishes. Both curly parsley and Italian parsley are perfect as a garnish.

117

ROSEMARY

Tender evergreen perennial
Height: 3 to 5 feet (90 to 150 cm)

Rosemary is a summer garden classic and a
basic herb to any kitchen. In the garden, it
is classified as a perennial, but because it is
such a tender plant, it is often grown as an
annual. Its 3 to 5 foot (90 to 150 cm) plantings make an interesting hedge or border
plant. When grown as a perennial, it
blooms with pale blue flowers. Like several
other popular herbs such as thyme and
mint, rosemary has several varieties.

In the Garden

Rosemary requires full sun and protection
from cold winds, as well as rich well-
drained, slightly moist soil. Sow under heat
in spring or outdoors in summer, although
rosemary propagates best by cuttings.
Transplant when large enough to handle
with 2 or 3 feet (60 to 90 cm) between
plants. To harvest, pick leaves in small
amounts any time. To preserve, dry sprigs
and branches, and then strip off the needle-
like leaves before storing.

© Derek Fell

*Rosemary, aromatic and
flavorful, adds a delicious
touch to chicken, as well as to
potatoes, tomatoes, zucchini,
and other vegetables.*

In the Kitchen

Use rosemary leaves to flavor virtually any
dish, from grilled meats—especially lamb
and pork—to chicken, fish, potatoes, vegetables, and even fresh fruits.

Tarragon

Hardy perennial
Height: 2 to 3 feet (60 to 90 cm)

Tarragon is one of the most important culinary herbs and together with chervil and parsley forms the basis for French fines herbes—and thus many French dishes. Tarragon has several varieties, but one of the most common is French tarragon, which has a refined, almost sweet flavor.

In the Garden

Tarragon requires a relatively sunny spot, sheltered from wind, and rich, light, dry soil. Tarragon must be grown from divisions or cuttings. Divide roots in spring, or take cuttings in summer, and thin to about 24 inches (60 cm) apart. Cut back in the fall and protect with straw in the winter. To harvest, pick leaves at any time. Dry, freeze, or infuse them in vinegar or oil.

In the Kitchen

Tarragon leaves provide a subtle sweet/savory fragrance and aroma to many dishes from soups and stews, to chicken, fish, and game dishes. Tarragon is not normally used for grilled or roasted meats, but it can provide a special flavor there, too.

Thymes

Perennial
Height: 3 to 18 inches (8 to 45 cm)

Thyme is one of the most ubiquitous herbal plants, boasting more than one hundred species and varieties, including *Thymus vulgaris,* common kitchen thyme. Thyme is an aromatic addition to the garden and an indispensable addition to the kitchen.

In the Garden

Thyme needs full sun and light, dry, well-drained soil. To propagate, start plants indoors and set them outside in spring spaced about 12 inches (30 cm) apart. To grow, thin or transplant if necessary to 9 to 15 inches (23 to 38 cm) apart, and prune frequently in summer. Thyme leaves dry or freeze well, but can also be infused in vinegar or oil.

In the Kitchen

Together with parsley and bay, thyme is part of the classic bouquet garni. It is an essential herb to any cook—particularly the French cook—and is a basic ingredient in many stocks, marinades, stuffings, sauces, and soups. With its pungent flavor, thyme is a delicious addition to poultry, fish, shellfish, vegetable, and game dishes.

Bouquet Garni

Makes 1 bouquet

The classic bouquet garni is used often in French cooking to flavor stews, soups, and sauces. Depending upon the dish, the bouquet garni can be varied to include appropriate herbs, but the one that follows is classic and suitable for most dishes. The herbs can be fresh or dried.

Classic bouquet garni:

2 sprigs parsley
1 bay leaf
¼ teaspoon thyme

Cut a small, 3-inch (8-cm) square of cheesecloth. Place the herbs in the center of the square, gather the edges, then wrap a length of string or twine around the bundle and knot it.

Herbes de Provence

Makes about ½ cup

There are many recipes for herbes de Provence because the herbs characteristic to Provence, France are numerous—including bay, basil, thyme, rosemary, savory, coriander, lavender, marjoram, and oregano—and the possibilities for delicious combinations are endless. The following is a simple recipe, very good for use on vegetables, as well as on grilled fish, in soups, and in stews. However, use your imagination and taste buds and design your own personal version of herbes de Provence.

2 tablespoons dried thyme leaves
1 tablespoon dried rosemary leaves
1 teaspoon dried tarragon leaves
1 teaspoon dried marjoram leaves
½ teaspoon dried lavender

Powder all the ingredients together in a blender, food processor, or by hand with a mortar and pestle. Store in an airtight container or plastic bag.

Herbed Butters

Herbed butters are almost essential for serving with freshly picked vegetables. Here are a few recipes for simple butters, but don't be afraid to create your own.

Basic recipe:

8 tablespoons (1 stick) unsalted butter,
    at room temperature
1 tablespoon lemon juice
Salt to taste
Freshly ground black pepper to taste
1 tablespoon chopped fresh parsley

Cream the butter, then beat in the remaining ingredients. Place the butter on a piece of plastic wrap and shape into a cylinder; or spoon into a crock and cover with plastic wrap. Chill.

This butter will stay fresh in the refrigerator for 2 weeks or will freeze for up to 3 months.

This is a good, basic herbed butter, delicious on fish and poultry, as well as vegetables.

Variations:

Variations to herbed butters are virtually infinite and depend upon the dishes you are cooking or your particular taste. Here are a few suggesions:

© Steven Mark Needham/Envision

Garlic butter: Add 2 minced cloves garlic to the basic recipe. Garlic butter is especially good on potatoes, toasted bread, or pasta.

Chive butter: Using the basic recipe, substitute chives for the parsley. This is particularly tasty with egg dishes or various vegetables.

Tarragon butter: Substitute tender young tarragon leaves, finely minced, for the parsley in the basic recipe. Tarragon is always delicious on chicken or fish.

Beurre de Provence: Substitute 1 finely minced shallot and 1 tablespoon of herbes de Provence for the parsley in the basic recipe.

Herbed butters can also be colored with beet juice or chopped spinach to create a festive touch.

121

GLOSSARY OF GARDENING TERMS

acid: A term applied to soil with a pH content of less than 6.5 that contains no lime. Most vegetables prefer a slightly acid soil.

alkaline: A term applied to soil with a pH content of more than 7.3.

annual: A plant that grows from seed, flowers, and then dies in one growing season. Most vegetables are annual.

biennial: A plant that takes two growing seasons to complete its life cycle.

bud: A young, undeveloped flower, although it can also denote a leaf or shoot.

bulb: A short stem that grows underground that contains food-storing leaves.

canning: A method of preserving foods, including vegetables.

compost: A blend of decomposed organic matter that is sometimes combined with soil or sand and used to nourish plants.

creeping: A term used to describe a plant that trails over the ground or over other plants.

crop rotation: Planting different species of plants in a particular area each season to prevent the soil from becoming depleted or diseased.

cross-pollination: The transfer of pollen from one plant to another.

cutting: A leaf, bud, or part of a stem or root without roots that is removed from a plant and potted to form the basis of a new plant.

division: To propagate by dividing roots or tubers into sections that are then replanted and form separate plants.

evergreen: A plant that bears living foliage all year-round.

drainage: The action or method of draining water from the garden plot or container.

drying: A method of preserving herbs, vegetables, seeds, and flowers by air-drying over a period of weeks.

freezing: A method of preserving foods, including vegetables.

fruit: The mature ovary of a flower that contains a seed or seeds.

genus (plural: genera): The classification of a group of closely related plants belonging to the same family.

germination: The moment a plant sprouts.

half-hardy: A term applied to annual plants indicating that they will grow outdoors but may not survive frost.

hardy: A term applied to plants indicating that they will tolerate freezing conditions and will survive a cold winter without protection.

herbaceous: A term usually applied to perennial plants whose stems are not woody and which die down at the end of each season.

humus: Partly or wholly decomposed vegetable matter that is used to nourish garden soil.

hybrid: A plant that results from a cross between two parent plants belonging to different species, subspecies, or genera.

legume: A member of the bean or pea family.

loam: Humus-rich soil containing up to 25 percent clay and less than 50 percent sand.

mulch: A covering—either organic or man-made—laid down to protect plant roots, hold moisture, control temperature, and control weeds.

peat moss: Partially decomposed moss, rich in nutrients and with high water retention capabilities, which is often added to garden soil to add nourishment to the soil.

perlite: A substance (literally a natural volcanic glass) used to enhance soilless media for starting seeds and cutting. Also added to garden soil to enhance drainage.

perennial: A plant that lives from year to year. The stems and leaves of a perennial die down in winter, but new shoots appear each spring.

pH scale: A system, measured on a scale of 1 to 14, devised to measure the acid/alkaline content of soil. Soils that register below 7 are acid; those above 7 are alkaline.

pinch: To remove leaves from a plant to encourage branching and richer growth.

pistil: The seed-bearing or female organ of a flower.

propagate: The process of reproducing plants.

prostrate: A term used to describe plants that creep, trail or lie on the ground.

rootstock: The crown and root system of herbaceous perennials and shrubs.

The term is also used to describe a vigorous plant onto which another plant is grafted.

runner: A stem that spreads along the soil surface, rooting wherever it comes into contact with moist soil, creating new plants.

seed: A fertilized ripened ovule that is contained in a fruit.

self-seed: A term applied to plants that drop their seeds around them from which new plants grow; self-sow.

shrub: A perennial whose stems and branches are woody and that grows only a few feet high.

species: A classification applied to plants from within a genus.

stamen: The male, pollen-bearing part of a flower.

thin: To weed out thickly planted growing areas and allow plants to grow with sufficient surrounding space. Plants may be removed and thrown away, or replanted elsewhere.

till: To work the soil into small fragments where seeds or seedlings can be planted.

tuber: A root or underground stem in which food is stored.

variety: A term applied to a naturally occurring variation of a species of plant.

vermiculite: A substance (literally any of a group of micaceous hydrate silicates) used together with peat moss and perlite to create a sterile soilless medium for starting seeds and cuttings.

weed: An unwanted plant in a lawn or garden. A rose bush may be considered a weed in a vegetable patch.

MAIL-ORDER SOURCES

The following are just a few of the many centers or companies across North America that supply seeds, plants, books, gardening accessories, and information. Write for a catalogue. Check in your local Yellow Pages under "Gardening Supplies" for suppliers in your area.

W. Atlee Burpee & Co.
Warminster, Pennsylvania 18974
or:
Clinton, Iowa 52732
or:
6350 Rutland Avenue
Box 748
Riverside, California 92502

Burpee's is perhaps the best-known supplier of seeds in the United States.

Brooklyn Botanic Garden
1000 Washington Avenue
Brooklyn, New York 11225

Comstock Ferre & Co.
263 Main Street
Wethersfield, Connecticut 06109

Cruickshank's Inc.
1015 Mt. Pleasant Road
Toronto, Ontario, Canada
M4P 2M1

Dominion Seed House, Ltd.
115 Guelph Street
Georgetown, Ontario, Canada
L7G 4A2

They have a comprehensive catalogue, but will ship only to Canadian addresses.

Gardener's Eden
P.O. Box 7307
San Francisco, California 94120

Exceptionally good-looking gardening supplies and accessories.

Gardenimport
P.O. Box 760
Thornhill, Ontario, Canada
L3T 4A5

Hancock Shaker Village
P.O. Box 898
Pittsfield, Massachusetts 01202

Jackson & Perkins
1 Rose Lane
Medford, Oregon 97501

A well-known supplier of roses, but they also have a seedbook with suggested vegetables.

Le Jardin du Gourmet
P.O. Box 31
West Danville, Vermont 05873

French varieties of vegetables, herbs, plants, and seeds.

Reuter Seed Co., Inc.
320 N. Carrolton Avenue
New Orleans, Louisiana 70119

An old and respected Southern seed supplier.

Williams-Sonoma
A Catalog for Cooks
P.O. Box 7456
San Francisco, California 04120-7456

SUGGESTED READING

Gardening Books

Brookes, John, *The Garden Book.* New York: Crown Publishers, Inc., 1984

Brookes, John, *The Indoor Garden Book.* New York: Crown Publishers, Inc., 1985

Brookes, John, *The Small Garden.* New York: Crown Publishers, Inc., 1989

Crockett, James Underwood, *Crockett's Victory Garden.* Boston: Little, Brown & Company, 1977

Crockett, James Underwood and Eds. of Time/Life Books, *The Time/Life Book of Vegetables and Fruits.* New York: Henry Holt, 1972

Doty, Walter L., *All About Vegetables.* San Francisco: Ortho Books, 1980

Halpin, Anne M., *The Window Box Book.* New York: Simon & Schuster, 1989

Larkom, Joy, *The Salad Garden.* New York: Penguin Books, 1984

McNair, James K., *The World of Herbs & Spices.* San Francisco: Ortho Books, 1978

Page, Mary and William T. Stern, *Culinary Herbs.* London: The Royal Horticultural Society, 1974

Reilly, Ann, Consulting Editor, *Taylor's Pocket Guide to Herbs and Edible Flowers.* Boston: Houghton Mifflin Company, A Chanticleer Press Edition, 1990

Reilly, Ann, Consulting Editor. *Taylor's Pocket Guide to Vegetables.* Boston: Houghton Mifflin Company, A Chanticleer Press Edition, 1990

Spoczynska, Joy O.I., *The Indoor Kitchen Garden.* New York: Harper & Row, 1989

Cookbooks

Anderson, Jean, *The Green Thumb Preserving Guide.* New York: William Morrow & Company, 1976

Bailey, Janet, *Keeping Food Fresh.* New York: Doubleday, 1985

Costner, Susan, *Good Friends, Great Dinners.* New York: Crown Publishers, Inc., 1987

Gubser, Mary, *Mary's Bread Basket and Soup Kettle.* New York: William Morrow & Company, 1974

Hadamuscin, John, *Special Occasions.* New York: Harmony Books, 1988

Holt, Geraldene, *Recipes from a French Herb Garden.* New York: Simon & Schuster, 1989

Johnson, Ronald, *The American Table.* New York: William Morrow & Company, 1984

Lang, Jenifer Harvey, *Tastings.* New York: Crown Publishers, Inc. 1986

Morash, Marian. *The Victory Garden Cookbook.* New York: Alfred A. Knopf, 1982

Owen, Millie, *A Cook's Guide to Growing Herbs, Greens, and Aromatics.* New York: Alfred A. Knopf, 1978

Rombauer, Irma S. and Marion Rombauer Becker, *Joy of Cooking.* Indianapolis: Bobbs Merrill Company, Inc., Current edition.

Schneider, Elizabeth, *Uncommon Fruits and Vegetables: A Commonsense Guide.* New York: Harper & Row, 1986

INDEX

Grateful acknowledgement is given to the following for use of their recipes in this book:

"Cabbage Stuffed with Mushrooms, Walnuts and Bulgur" and "Tomato-Caraway Coulis" by Susan Costner. © 1987 by Susan Costner. By permission of Crown Publishers, Inc.

"Roasted Brook Trout with Tomato, Zucchini & Basil" © 1990 by Chef Waldy Malouf, The Hudson River Club, New York City.